T0381026

Worthy: The Power of Kindness in Raising Body Positive Children

Self-love is the basis of healthy relationships in life and is a teaching that most children do not receive. Every parent should read this book to provide their child with the foundations of self-love for success in all aspects of their life, which is the wish of every parent. Full of invaluable information, it acts as a manual for teaching children to be healthy and happy in body, mind, and spirit from a place of compassion, kindness, and support. Worthy also provides parents an opportunity to become more self-aware of their own misconceptions and conditioned beliefs, thereby allowing for their own evolution and growth along the way. This book is a rare gem!

Sheila Patel, MD
Chief Medical Officer, Chopra Global
Board-certified Family Physician

So many parents are searching for ways to teach their children how to love themselves from the inside-out, but it's hard to know who to trust for advice. As a mom of two young daughters myself, I feel this pain in a real way— the fear that our kids might one day be teased or bullied about the way they look; the worry that they will internalize the media's "be thin at all costs" message or learn from their friends that it's okay to weaponize the word "fat." Stevelos offers a fresh perspective to body positivity, with actionable strategies for keeping children feeling healthy, safe, loved, and, yes, worthy.

–Leslie Goldman, MPH
Women's health writer, body image speaker

Childhood obesity and overweight are on the rise and the causes are complicated and misunderstood. JoAnn Stevelos outlines the many underlying causes of obesity and sets the record straight, throwing a life preserver to parents who may be drowning in misinformation.
Often, parents feel judged by their child's pediatrician, coach, or other parents, and resort to methods like putting kids on keto diets or restricting portions at meals. Instead, *Worthy* helps teach parents and caregivers how to support children with esteem-building actions and phrases of kindness, while learning how to address the fat-shaming practices in their child's world – from overt bullying at school to being called "chubby" by grandparents to the subtle yet embarrassing practice of stepping on a scale in the pediatrician's office. Self-reflection activities throughout the book teach parents and caregivers how to turn conversations around from fat-shaming to esteem-building in a non-judgmental way.

–Anastasia Schepers, MS, RDN, CDN, CLC

JoAnn Stevelos has crafted a wonderfully comprehensive look at the factors causing the spike in obesity in this country, particularly in our children. She has done so thoughtfully with an eye toward kindness in coping with this epidemic. Too often obesity triggers blame which in turn fuels the cycle of shame and a sense of hopelessness, neither of which are helpful in leading a full and healthy life. As she writes: "The spirit of this book is to prioritize your own and your children's happiness, safety, well being and to protect your hope for a better future together" and the words she's penned, the research she shares, does just that. Sadly, as she details, this generation of children will not enjoy a life expectancy greater than their parents due to many factors including obesity. Add into this mix the trauma triggered by the pandemic. Taken together it's clear that being gentle with each other, with ourselves must be the front line approach, the elixir we all need to find our way back to a healthy lifestyle, one that includes our physical, mental and spiritual needs. It helps us develop a sense of being worthy to enjoy all life has to offer, to be strong enough to weather what life brings us and to carve out a path that supports our well being. In the end it's not about the size of the waistline, but the breadth of our kindness. Stevelos shares this 'prescription' mixed with a healthy dose of delight. A must read for anyone raising a child (children) or nurturing their own, inner child.
–Benita Zahn, DPS, MS, CHWC

Navigating conversations about body image can be incredibly hard for any parent. *Worthy* teaches a powerful set of tools that will help you nurture a healthy relationship between your child and their body.
–Evan Walden, CEO, Getro Inc.

Every child is worthy of a body positive home, school, and medical environment. Using the power of kindness is the best way to create safe spaces for children of all sizes and shapes!
–Akerei Maresala-Thomson, MBA | Founder Institute and CEO of MYRIVR

This book offers hope and great insights into the power of kindness in raising children to have a positive attitude towards their bodies, both now and in the future. We wish every parent had a copy of *Worthy* to read when we were growing up. Truly inspirational!
–Elia Chan, MBA-- Founder-Managing Director of MYRIVR
GROUP LTD-T/A MYRIVR Technologies

Our team of experts has been delving into the relationship between mental health and its impact on school violence. Since the conclusion of the coronavirus pandemic, we've come across reports highlighting the adverse effects on students' lives. With a noticeable increase in violence within schools, we are actively exploring the most effective methods to ensure the safety of both students and staff. One crucial approach involves teaching children about their inherent worth from a young age and fostering a general respect for all life. Worthy guides children to embrace a healthy and joyful lifestyle in body, mind, and spirit, while cultivating a mindset of compassion and kindness. This represents the cultural shift and emphasis on mental health that we believe will make a positive impact on safety and security within schools and for today's youth as a whole.
–Elisa Mula, Physical Security Strategist, Child Safety & Security Advocate

CONTENTS

Introduction

THE TRANSFORMATIVE
POWER OF KINDNESS

Be kind whenever possible. It is always possible.

—The 14th Dalai Lama

How do we help children who have gained too much weight too fast feel cared for, loved, and safe? How do we prevent children from experiencing fat-shaming, weight bias, and bullying in our culture? How do we compassionately and kindly care for children who are going through changes in their weight? The Covid-19 pandemic has magnified the problem of gaining too much weight too fast for children and adults. Stress, inactivity, comfort eating, and increased screen time made it relatively easy to gain 20-30 lbs, the average excess weight gain reported by pediatricians. *Worthy* is a parent's guide to help you understand your feelings about weight, help you understand how you perceive your child's weight, and show you how to help your child to be their healthiest self.

As someone who has spent over 20 years working all over the US and internationally in leadership roles, including directing the New York State Center for Best Practices to Prevent Childhood Obesity and evaluating Michelle Obama's Let's Move program and the Alliance for a Healthier Generation's childhood obesity programs, I've talked at length with doctors, parents, teachers, health insurers, policymakers, researchers, and scientists about the childhood obesity epidemic. I have learned so much about how to help children and parents who struggle daily with embarrassing, stigmatizing conditions and are ashamed to ask anyone or seek professional help. I am inspired and committed to sharing what I have learned about weight issues during the childhood obesity epidemic so that children and families can stop suffering in silence. In *Worthy*, you will learn how to create a safe space for your child and receive the help and resources they need to have a healthy and happy childhood. I want to give parents hope because I know how to help.

While some researchers disagree over whether parents and doctors should discuss weight-related issues with children, I share the opinion of a growing number of experts that we should speak with children about gaining too much weight too fast. When we fail to kindly and compassionately discuss children's weight changes, we are simply not helping them. Our silence does not protect children from bullying, feelings of unworthiness, or social isolation. What is most concerning is the relationship between bullying and suicide, especially in children who have gained too much weight too fast. Children who are victims of weight-related teasing or bullying are 2-3 times more likely to report thoughts of suicide or to engage in self-harming behavior, such as self-cutting. What an alarming statistic.

Worthy will help families use the power of kindness to create body-positive environments at home, school, and the doctor's office. Healing our sense of worthiness and our children's worthiness is emotional work that requires open, loving hearts to dissolve the shame and set productive boundaries. *Worthy* uses the best research and tools to help families build body-positive, loving homes filled with kindness and joy. Dads have told me, "This is embarrassing, but why does my eight-year-old son have breasts?" Moms are worried about early puberty and how they can protect their nine-year-old who just started menstruation and has the body of a developing preteen.

The big secret is that researchers and experts know that obesity isn't a willpower problem; it's a physiological problem. Starving somebody thin works temporarily, but the body is too smart. It will eventually take over by lowering metabolism and increasing hunger. Getting medical help for a child gaining too much weight too fast isn't taking the easy way out -- it may be the only way out. Parents need guidance on finding the right doctor, talking to medical professionals in a way that will help their child, and showing clinicians they are serious about helping their child. Many parents want to address the underlying medical conditions causing too much weight gain too fast in their child and get sustained support so their child can get better. Children dealing with weight changes need resilient, compassionate advocates. During this obesity pandemic, some parents may need to become their family's obesity experts.

Worthy will encourage you to keep searching and keep hopeful until you find the right combination of things to help your child and yourself feel more confident and capable. We can do better for our children—we must—the consequences are too significant—the risk of having even one child going through weight changes feel unloved or unsafe is unacceptable. ***You and your child are worthy of loving-kindness.***

[1]

Choose Joy For You and Your Child

There comes a time in the spiritual journey when you start making choices from a very different place. And if a choice lines up so that it supports truth, health, happiness, wisdom, and love, it's the right choice.

—Angeles Arrien (1940-2015) Anthropologist

When I read this quote, I thought, this is what compassion for the self looks like. When we think about ourselves from a place of compassion, we support a healthier, kinder, loving place to live. Everything I have learned about healing from the negative experiences related to childhood obesity through my research and interviews with parents, doctors, teachers, and policymakers comes back to compassion for yourself and your child. Without it, the world is a lonely place where you and your child feel vulnerable and abandoned. Learning to have compassion and kindness for yourself as the caregiver will help you better understand what your child needs from you.

Compassion for yourself is about respecting, accepting, and choosing joy for yourself and your child. It is easier to act on this when we understand what compassion is not:

Compassion is not about white lies and hiding the truth. When we conceal the truth from ourselves and the people we interact with, it prevents us from being fully present and living without fear.

Compassion is not conditional. Putting conditions on whether or not we love ourselves or our child prevents us from engaging in love and joy. Conditional love sounds like this: "I will be happy when I lose 20 pounds or when my child is thinner." "If only my child could get past this abuse, we would all be happier." If you're waiting for happiness to come to you and your child, you're putting conditions on your own and your child's joy.

Compassion for yourself is not self-pity. We all know people like Eeyore in the Winnie the Pooh stories. Eeyores tend to think in absolutes—either it is good or it is terrible. People who feel sorry for themselves don't see the shades of gray as opportunities to change their environment or behavior. Compassion for you and your child is about having the confidence to accept yourself in every way, every day and seek ways to change the environment or the behavior to make yourself and your child more comfortable.

Compassion for yourself is not overly generous; it does not overlook your mistakes. Looking at one's behavior or thoughts with kindness is to accept that we are human, make mistakes, and are not perfect. Being honest and looking within yourself can help you understand when you should say no to things not aligned with your commitment to finding balance and joy in your life.

When we spend our lives waiting to be happy or feel joy until we are a perfect size, weight, or fit into a dress or jeans, we are sacrificing our ability to live our true potential and share our gift of love and friendship in the world. We lose our opportunity to participate fully in a meaningful way - in our unique way. Even when we know intellectually that no one is perfect and that there is always someone smarter, thinner, funnier, or more beautiful than ourselves, we often let an image we hold as ideal diminish our compassion for ourselves and our children. Because of our weight, we may feel less than others and perceive our children with rapid weight changes as having something wrong with them, something to be fixed. Rather than sitting on the sidelines feeling imperfect, wishing to disappear because of our size or shape, we need to view ourselves and our children from a distance - from a place where love and compassion see only your heart, intention, and vulnerability. From this distant place, you can begin to experience the necessary empathy and worthiness to let your true self be seen, the best self you are on this day, at this time, for this purpose.

I hope you will begin to experience compassion, worthiness, and joy as we explore the answers to these questions:

Why are weight changes affecting my family? What made us vulnerable to gaining too much weight too fast?

What keeps us from being tender, loving, and kind to ourselves?

How are we outwardly reflecting or accepting these feelings of unworthiness and shame to our children?

How do our children perceive our attitudes towards ourselves, body shape, and health?

How am I protecting myself and my children from fat-shaming and weight bias?

Why is my child developing early?

What is weight bias? How do I deal with weight bias at home, school, and doctor's offices?

Worthy will help you understand that there are many reasons your child may be gaining weight too fast and are not within your child's or your control.

[2]

Acceptance At Any Weight, Busting the Obesity Myth

There's no prerequisites to worthiness. You're born worthy, and I think that's a message a lot of women need to hear.

–Viola Davis

I have heard many stories about how parents feel, think, and obsess over their own weight and their family members' weight. I'd say, in general, there seem to be two camps of parents. Parents who worry about their weight don't want their children to weigh the same as them. And parents who gave up and accepted their size. These parents often said things like, "Hey, we're just big people. Of course, my child is big. He looks just like his dad." A familiar feeling in both camps is that neither felt worthy of acceptance, just as they were— whatever size they were. It didn't occur to many people I spoke with that it is not about personal failure. It might not just be about them and what they are doing or not doing. Then who is to blame? Schools? Parents? TV? Big Food? Video Games?

There's an old saying, "You can't boil the ocean." So don't worry. I am not even going to try. It's nearly impossible to connect the dots that led to the obesity epidemic and all its co-existing conditions like type 2 diabetes, hypertension, and sleep apnea. I am pretty sure that if you picked up this book, you just want to help your child. You don't want a crash course in how changing agricultural policies, genetics, geography, prenatal exposure to endocrine disruptors, and a bunch of other reasons led us to this obesity epidemic. Typically each new generation lives longer than their parents. Today, this generation of children will not live as long as their parents have lived. So yeah, this is frightening and heartbreaking.

In our world today, people are gaining too much weight too fast despite a gazillion magazines telling us how to exercise more and eat less sugar, salt, and fat—or telling us to eat more fat and protein and fewer carbs—the keto diet. Or to fast intermittently. Or to take this supplement while drinking big glasses of fresh-pressed, expensive juice. But here's where it gets tricky. To begin to feel worthy of acceptance at any size, I think it is important to understand just a few things about obesity. These things will help you understand what obesity is and why it is a metabolic disorder, not a personal failure. I want to help you to stop blaming yourself. There is so much we don't understand about obesity and why it affects some people and not others. But the things we do understand can help you shift your thinking, shift your perspective and perhaps be a little gentler and kinder to yourself and your child.

Meanwhile, we first need to understand that the weight epidemic is bigger than all of us. The research thus far has not produced a magic pill that is safe for children, a way of eating, or a way to prevent it in the first place that works for every person suffering from obesity. So be patient for a few paragraphs while I cover what we know about obesity and a few big things we are trying to understand.

First, did you know that more people live with "extreme obesity" than HIV, breast cancer, Alzheimer's, and Parkinson's disease? That's insane, right? More than breast cancer! The obesity epidemic started 30 to 40 years ago and has brought us to the current time when one in three children and 75 percent of adults are overweight or obese. It is rare now to meet a family in the US that has not been affected by this epidemic. Well, what the heck is happening? Why are people getting so big? And why does it matter? Even though we know people are talking or worried about their weight all the time, we researchers are not coming up with many good ideas for families. But what we have done well is ring the bell. Around 2007, we told people, hey; there is an obesity epidemic. Parents of children ages 0-5 were told to do XYZ, so their children didn't become part of the epidemic. XYZ included switching babies from whole milk to 2% at age two, limiting fruit juice and soda, getting kids active for at least 60 minutes per day, and so on. These recommendations did help, after several years, to keep the obesity rates in children from increasing. But one in three children with obesity still needs our help now.

Children get older, habits are formed, and the 10-year-old who gained too much weight too fast and didn't lose the weight by the time they are a young adult will have a challenging time losing weight—ever. Why? Because habits are formed early, because their bodies will always carry the same fat cells, or because exposure to endocrine disruptors (like pesticides) has altered their metabolism in ways we don't understand. The fact is, there is no single reason!

When we look at things that cause obesity, we look at causes that are inside the person and causes that are outside the person. There are many things inside the person that are potential contributors to obesity. Some make us eat more, and some make us move less. There is an interplay between psychological factors, biological makeup, and environmental pressures. Factors may include hyper-reactivity to environmental food cues, heightened hunger response, delayed satiety, age-related changes (menopause, hormones), thyroid dysfunction, chronic inflammation, and so on. Pair one of these biological factors with psychological issues like a history of trauma, mental impairments, depression, or anxiety, and you have the perfect storm for weight changes because of cortisol. Cortisol is a hormone that our body produces when we are stressed. It is one of the main contributors to weight changes.

When looking for potential contributors outside the person, we see that the research is all over the board. However, we have identified approximately 45 external factors that influence the number you see on the scale. The main one is focused on your mother. No, we are not blaming mothers for the obesity epidemic. But some people deeply entrenched in patriarchal culture say it is women's fault. The start of the obesity epidemic coincides with the dawn of the feminist revolution. As a result, some people will falsely argue that "Mom went to work and the kids gained too much weight." Other people falsely claim that obesity is the unintended consequence of anti-smoking campaigns. This is even more ridiculous. But in the absurd, we can sometimes find a grain of truth. Mothers do have something to do with the obesity epidemic, but it is really due to what happens during a woman's pregnancy. Did she have a stressful pregnancy? Was she exposed to pollution? Did she delay getting prenatal care? Did she have a C-section? The list is too long to cite here, but you get the point.

The second biggest potential factor outside the person that may cause obesity is our food environment. Families are not eating together, eating away from home, skipping meals, and being given huge portions. Also, there is a lot of energy-dense food available wherever we go. Do we need chips, soda, and candy available at hardware stores? Can't we shop for paint or a hammer without being tempted to eat snacks that are far from healthy?

The final categories of potential contributors to obesity are your social life, how much money you make, and where you live. If your friends and family engage in physical activity and eat healthily, you are more likely to do the same. Where we live greatly influences our health. If you have enough money for healthcare, healthy foods, and living somewhere with access to a safe physical environment, you are much more likely to be healthier. Typically, people are healthier when they live in walkable communities with access to fresh, healthy foods and minimal pollution.

Phew—you made it through the boring stuff! I hope you take away this—many things have made you and your family vulnerable to the obesity epidemic. It is not personal. It is not your fault. And throughout this book, I will remind you that you are worthy of acceptance, joy, kindness, and love, just as you are at whatever size.

Before we talk about why we can gain too much weight too fast, let's agree that we won't judge ourselves against a standard produced by a fashion magazine or the images we have collected in our minds about how we should look. For simplicity, our purpose here is to think about what you and your child's healthiest weight could be and how the right amount of rest, sleep, fuel, exercise, support, and kindness will help you both feel your best.

As a society, we revere thinness. However, we turn a blind eye to all the harm the marketing of thinness causes. One thing we do is measure ourselves against unrealistic expectations. We compare ourselves to others and track how we are doing based on an expectation we have established in our minds. Essentially, we are trying to gauge our worthiness around particular parameters. Labeling ourselves as "not thin" lets marketers and pseudo-fitness industries off the hook as part of the problem. But the culture of thinness that they sell and the messages that they use hurt all of us. It makes those of us not struggling with our weight changes susceptible to false beliefs like, "Heavy people are lazy," or "All they have to do is eat healthily and move more, and they will be an acceptable size," or "How did they let themselves go?" These false beliefs about rapid weight changes or obesity make people act less compassionately and less kind. They exhibit what we researchers call weight bias. Weight bias is when you judge someone's character or inherent nature based on their size or how much flesh is on their bones. We all suffer when you judge someone by how much they weigh and not who they are. Weight bias gets in the way of true connectedness. The positive relationships that foster positive environments and a sense of community for all people.

Weight bias hurts us all. And it especially hurts our children. Have you thought you are less of a good parent because of how much you or your child weighs? Please don't judge yourself as a parent. Just introduce the idea of how the culture of thinness has affected you and your child. Remember, there are a host of reasons that some children gain too much weight too fast. And not all of them are in our control. This leads us to the idea of worthiness. You and your child are worthy of love, kindness, and compassion. Read this sentence as many times as you need to feel the words, to feel them in your heart and your mind. When we connect our minds and body, we can genuinely build hope, resilience, and the deep love and security we all need to thrive.

Worthiness

Have you ever stopped thinking about how lucky you are to have your body? Seriously! Think about it! Your body is fantastic. It is a complex organism that can withstand a snowstorm. And yet, exposure to one little cold germ can put us in bed for a week. Our bodies can eat hundreds of different foods, breathe in millions of different particles, move in and out of positions without much thought, and run virtually every major internal organ without even thinking about it. We sometimes do a lot of things to abuse our bodies, like drinking alcohol, taking drugs, overeating, working out too long, not dealing with our stress, or staying up late binging on TV. Despite our lack of care, our body keeps on working for us. When was the last time you thanked your legs for bringing you home, your arms for carrying groceries, your lungs for taking in oxygen, or your heart for pumping 2,000 gallons of blood on any given day? Our bodies work hard and are worthy of love, gratitude, and kindness.

The more we learn how to take better care of our bodies and understand how our mind and body are connected, our bodies will better care for ourselves. Our bodies and our children's bodies are worthy of good, healthy foods that help us grow and perform at our best. We deserve foods that nourish us and help us feel good about ourselves, making our thoughts feel welcome about what we ate, not guilt or shame. The information below was compiled from many studies. However, the primary sources are the Center for Disease Control and the National Institute of Health.

Our Metabolism

We all would like obesity to be as simple as our metabolism is slow and would love to be given a prescription to speed it up. Your metabolism helps regulate your body's primary energy needs. Metabolism is all about how our bodies convert food into energy. This is a reasonably complex process. Here is a simple explanation: what we eat and drink combines oxygen to release our body's energy to function.

Even when resting, our body needs energy for all its "hidden" functions, such as breathing, circulating blood, adjusting hormone levels, and growing and repairing cells. The number of calories our bodies use to carry out their "hidden" functions is called our basal metabolic rate — or our metabolism.

Several things give us our basal metabolic rate, including our body size. If we are big, tall, and muscular, we burn more calories, even when resting. Another factor is our sex. Men typically have less body fat and muscle than women of the same age and weight, meaning men burn more calories. This is good for men but may be annoying for women. Our age plays a significant role in our basal metabolic rate too. As we get older, we lose muscle, which slows down our rate of burning calories.

In addition to our basal metabolic rate, two other factors determine how many calories our bodies burn daily. The first is how bodies process food, called thermogenesis. This means we use energy to digest food— about 10 percent of the calories from the carbohydrates and proteins we eat are used to digest our food, send it through our body, and are absorbed as nutrients.

The second factor is physical activity, which also affects our basal metabolic rate. That is no surprise to most of us. The more we move, the more calories we burn, and the more muscle we develop; this helps us burn more calories, even when resting. And then, we have something called non-exercise activity thermogenesis (NEAT). We burn calories from doing simple things, like getting dressed in the morning, walking around the house, straightening up, or getting the mail.

Now that we understand how our metabolism works and how wondrous it is to digest food and produce the energy needed to do things that keep us alive, it is less tempting to blame our metabolism for weight gain. Our metabolism is not why most adults and children gain too much weight too fast. However, some exceptions exist, such as Cushing's syndrome or hypothyroidism. Weight gain is a complicated process. We believe it is most likely to be a combination of our genes, how our hormones work, what we eat, where we live, how much sleep we get, how much exercise, and how much stress we have in our lives. By understanding how much work your body does to give you the energy to live, you will hopefully gain a new perspective. Your body and your child's body are ***worthy*** of your respect, love, and kindness. Maybe, even a giant thank you.

Our Heart

Our hearts beat over 100,000 times per day. Our hearts pump 2,000 gallons of oxygen-rich blood to every cell in our body. Our hearts need us to help them by learning how to deal with stress and threats in our lives. Our hearts are critical to understanding how to best care for ourselves and our children in the obesity epidemic.

We must tend to our hearts. We must nurture and care for our hearts tenderly and with compassion. The obesity epidemic has created many places that leave our children and us feeling unwelcome, unloved, like outsiders. We need to reclaim our loving tenderness towards ourselves and our children and set firm boundaries around the kind of words we use about our bodies or our children's bodies. Loneliness, isolation, and hopelessness can damage or weaken our hearts and make them work harder to pump blood. Love, kindness, compassion, and tenderness provide the best fuel to help our hearts do their job.

How do we care for our hearts and our children's hearts? By committing ourselves to set boundaries that protect ourselves and our children from harmful environments, people, and events. We care by speaking kindly to ourselves and our children about our bodies and shifting how others talk about our size and our children's size. Our hearts need us to focus on the things we do well, the things that make us feel loved, the things that bring us joy and contentment. Our hearts need us and our children to be our healthiest selves and weight. What do I mean by your child's healthiest weight and shape?

Your child's healthiest weight and shape is when they meet these 5 criteria:

1. Have a best friend.
2. Sleep well.
3. Move the way they want, when they want.
4. Feel comfortable and safe at home, going to school, and at the doctor's office.
5. Choose to eat healthy foods 80% of the time.

When we create environments that support these five things, whatever that number is on the scale, and what our child's body size or shape is, that is who they are. And that child, your child, is ***worthy*** of loving-kindness, compassion, and a joyful life.

Our Brain

Why do we get hungry? Because our brains work to keep our energy levels stable to keep our body working. We start to feel hungry as soon as our stomachs are empty. But why do we still want to snack or crave a piece of chocolate if we have just finished dinner? There are two kinds of hunger. One type of hunger—homeostatic—is all about balancing our energy reserves in the short term. The other type of hunger—hedonic—wants to gather extra energy. Researchers know very little about hedonic hunger. They know that our eyes play a significant role in why we will be tempted to eat donuts at 10 AM even if we had a healthy breakfast at 8 AM. Our brain is notified when our eyes detect something we have previously enjoyed eating. If we are full, we might be able to avoid eating the donut. However, because our brains are hardwired to avoid running out of energy, the sight of extra food can override our feeling of fullness and give the wrong signal that we need the extra food because we might run out of energy.

This is just one theory about why we overeat. And this is why it is always hard to eat healthily. The food environment we live in constantly tempts us with extra food that creates an internal argument with our brains. We are trying to tell it, "I don't want to eat the donut," and our brain is saying, "You saw the donut, and we need extra food in case there is no food later." As we understand the brain's role, we can be more compassionate to ourselves and our children. We can learn to reassure our brain that we have eaten a healthy meal and are in no danger of starving or running out of energy. And maybe, you can give the brain a big thanks for caring, but you got this one.

Reflecting and cultivating a sense of worthiness

Food and sadness are old friends. Many of us turn to food for comfort or offer food to our children when they feel sad. Now that we understand how and why we become hungry, we can better understand how we may help ourselves and our children find comfort elsewhere. This idea of comfort food is all around us. Movies and TV shows constantly refer to comfort foods. We see recipes for comfort foods on the front covers of national magazines. Let me be clear. I am not against comfort foods. I love my mac and cheese when I feel sad about something on a cold February night. And if I am that awful kind of crying sad, I may add a few breadcrumbs to the top and maybe some hot sauce too. There is nothing wrong with comfort food on occasions that we need extra care, like a death in the family, the loss of a job, recovering from trauma, or just having a bad day at work. But an occasion is just that, a one-time event that happens infrequently.

When we eat comfort foods every day, we can suffer from heartburn, constipation, or stomach aches. Our bodies do not perform well when we eat heavily processed foods. And when we turn to comfort food every day for comfort, we will begin to feel sick and maybe even sadder. The comfort food may feel good while we eat it, but within an hour or two, we may start to feel ill. Can you think of a time this happened to you? To your child?

How do we stop the cycle of using food for comfort or offering food as comfort to our children? One way is to take a few minutes to understand your or your child's feelings. Ask yourself or your child—what is hurting? Is your heart sad because someone said an unkind thing? Is your spirit hurting because you feel lonely? What needs comfort? Then try to find another way to provide comfort. How about a hug? Watching a movie? Would a trip to the playground help? And for you, what would help comfort you when you feel lonely, tired, or stressed?

Surprise Yourself With New Comforts

Finding new ways to comfort ourselves is like a surprise gift. As we find new ways to relax or revisit old habits, like taking a hot bath or calling an old friend just to chat, our brain will connect the new way of comforting and rewarding us by feeling less stress and, hopefully, comfort. We don't need to find big things to comfort us. Small things work best. Maybe you can give your child a special stone or necklace to help calm them and remind them of your love and support. Perhaps we listen to a song that uplifts us and helps spark joy in us. Can you remember a time that you felt comforted by something? Can you think of a few new ways to comfort your child when they need your love and support?

One of many ways we caregivers can help our children is to begin to feel worthy and uncover hope for ourselves. We know that children learn the most from what we say and do consistently. The next chapter will examine how we feel about ourselves and our child's size and shape. We will learn how our shame can affect our children's sense of shame. And we will learn some slight shifts in thinking and actions that can help us begin to reignite hope, compassion, love, and joy in our lives. Whether it is actively changing how we speak about our weight, our child's weight, or the shape of our bodies, or by cultivating healthy eating and activity habits, we can learn to take the first steps to improve our health and happiness.

Five things researchers know about children gaining too much weight too fast:

1. They eat more calories than they burn.
2. Their diets have a lot of processed foods and sweetened beverages.
3. They spend more than two hours per day watching television, texting, playing video games, and sitting in front of a computer.
4. Their parents struggle with gaining too much weight too fast.
5. They sleep poorly.

Some questions researchers are studying about why children are gaining too much weight too fast:

1. Does exposure to pesticides disrupt a child's growth and cause early puberty and growth disturbances?
2. Do food additives, such as animal growth hormones, affect children's growth?
3. Do growth hormones given to cows transfer to humans through beef and milk consumption?
4. What role have agricultural policy changes played over the past thirty years in the childhood obesity epidemic? Did the shift to corn and high fructose foods impact children's weight?
5. Can system and policy changes at schools change a child's weight? For example, schools increase the number of recess hours and serve healthy snacks.
6. Does early antibiotic use (before 18 months) affect children's weight?
7. Does the age and weight of the mothers affect children's weight?
8. Does where a child lives affect that child's weight? Can children walk to school or a local park?

[3]

Our Fat-Shaming Culture and Combating Shame

*Those who feel lovable, who love, and who experience belonging
simply believe they are worthy of love and belonging.*

–Brene Brown

One day, not too long ago, I watched my lifelong friend Peter snap at a nurse who had come into his room for the umpteenth time to take his temperature. He was in the final days of his life and couldn't understand why anyone would need to know if his body was running hot or cold. He winced when he saw the expressions on my face–surprise and embarrassment. Peter took a deep breath and said, "Jo, sometimes you just have to teach people how to treat you—and you better start soon. Stop being so polite all the time. Speak up." And he was right. The nurse apologized and didn't come back until the next day. And following Peter's advice, that is what we will do here—give you the words and a few actions to teach people how to treat you and your child. Establish some boundaries.

We know that nearly half of adults—half the people you talk to daily—are worried about gaining weight or not losing weight fast enough. Sadly, those who study kids and weight gain have learned that almost half of girls 3-6 years old are conscious of their weight and have shared with researchers that they 'don't want to get fat.' More alarming was a recent study that explored how girls feel about too much weight gain. The researchers had children as young as five years old enrolled in the study! What in the world is happening when five-year-old girls are part of a National Institute of Health study to determine whether they worry about gaining weight? That our children are this vulnerable to the fat-shaming culture is heartbreaking.

Over the years, I have listened to many people share their deepest feelings about their and their children's weight. Feelings about weight gain and weight loss are deeply embedded in our personal histories. These feelings can bring on bouts of depression, shame, and hopelessness. Many of us have lost our ability, our armor, to protect our sense of self from feeling less than or unworthy.

I am a co-crier by nature. If you cry, I cry too. I teared up when, during parent interviews, I saw a painful memory resurface that caused a quiver in their voice. I watched them stop and look away—not ready to share—still feeling shame or embarrassment. Sometimes a parent squinted away tears when they remembered a name they were called or a sharp word from a sibling. Sometimes they repeated the word and winced, recognizing as an adult how awful it was to be called that as a child. Their pain is still very real. In The Body Keeps the Score, Bessel Van Der Kolk tells us, "we remember insults and injuries best: The adrenaline that we secrete to defend against potential threats helps engrave those incidents into our minds. Even though the content of the remark fades, our dislike for the person who made it usually persists."

When we instinctively shy away from using fat-shaming language and try to approach the subject gently, we are showing our emotional intelligence and our love for our child. Many of us avoid using words like 'fat,' 'obese,' or 'overweight' when discussing a child's weight. We often use words like 'big or 'heavy' and refer to the whole family as such. 'We are big people,' or, "Our family has always been on the heavy side." Sometimes we affectionately speak of our child's size as in, "She's always been my chunky monkey," or "He's my little chubster."

Because obesity is a complex problem, we must be cautious when we accept easy answers for why children are gaining weight rapidly. Suppose we believe obesity is simply due to eating too much and not exercising enough. In that case, we blame the children and, more often, the parents. We must consider all the reasons that cause children to gain too much weight too quickly. Most studies have found that weight, overweight, or obesity should not be discussed with or in front of children younger than eight. With all its variables and complexities, a younger child cannot understand how weight is gained. More importantly, younger children are dependent entirely on their parents.

Many parents try to help a child who is gaining too much weight quickly and fails. Worrying, nagging, nudging, food policing, and screen time monitoring usually end in arguments and hurt feelings. Often we are worried about our weight too. We may feel guilt, shame, and a sense of unworthiness because of our body shape. Everywhere we turn, we are told too much weight will cause diseases like diabetes and hypertension. As we try to make the right choices for ourselves and our children, there is always a lingering feeling that we haven't done enough, are not good enough, or do not have enough time. Another day has ended, and we have failed to live up to the ideal of providing three healthy meals, keeping a clean house, having a productive workday, getting to the gym, or exercising with our children.

As I see it, if you are trying to parent in this obesity crisis and Covid-19 pandemic, you are probably overwhelmed. We are told, don't eat this, eat that, limit screen time, move more, talk to your child about their weight, and don't talk to your child about their weight changes. What seems like conflicting advice comes from many different sources. While we know that some childhood obesity prevention efforts are promising, many do not work.

In a 2018 study published in the British Medical Journal, researchers studied 1,169 first-graders in 53 British primary schools for 30 months. They were part of a program to help children and their families live healthier lifestyles. The families participated in healthy cooking classes and healthy eating, and the children had 30 extra minutes to play during school. But even with all that, nothing changed. No significant change in weight occurred despite families loving the program, children getting to play more, and everyone eating healthier. That is the bad news. The good news is that learning healthier behaviors may decrease their risk for other weight-related diseases like type 2 diabetes or hypertension.

We can also think about this study in another way. We now know what doesn't work, so we must try something different to solve this complex problem of children gaining and keeping too much weight too fast. We need new strategies and ideas. And while we all try to figure this out, let's be kind to one another. Let's support one another and hope for solutions. There is hope. There is a new day, the next day.

There is a way for us to talk with love, compassion, and kindness about gaining too much weight too fast. There is a way to feel worthy and compassionate towards ourselves and our children of any size, at any weight. Parenting children in this obesity and pandemic crisis, we must pay attention and stay engaged. Embracing our imperfections as parents allow our children to see us make mistakes, learn from them, and try again. It helps you and your child build hope, resilience, and courage to keep trying to make healthy choices, be active, and find the simple joys of having meaningful and deep connections at home, school, and in their communities.

The good news is that the number of children with too much weight gain was leveling off before the COVID-19 pandemic. The number of children with too much weight gain has remained reasonably stable at about 17% affecting approximately 12.7 million children and adolescents. The not-so-good news is that there are 12.7 million children who continue to struggle with gaining too much weight too fast. Many are seriously ill and need safe, effective, compassionate care.

Clinicians and public health professionals often use body mass index (BMI) to determine obesity. Let's talk about the history of BMI for just a minute. It is a public health and research tool and not a tool for parents to assess their child's health. Here's why. First, Adolphe Quetelet created the body mass index in the 19th century. Quetelet created BMI as a tool to assess weight distribution across populations. He based his idea of "the ideal man" using the measurements of white, male Scottish and French soldiers. Later in the 1970s, a few important US-based doctors got frustrated with insurance companies arbitrarily setting weight and death standards to get their insurance payments. The US-based doctors rebranded Quetelet's index for use in the United States. Other countries also adopted the BMI standard even though it used the measurements of white men. Despite its questionable history and implicit racism, BMI is how we measure health for all races, genders, and body types.

Creating a safe space for all children to share their worries, fears, and experiences with compassionate, loving listeners is essential to helping them feel like the world can be kind, that they belong, and that they are loved. Children with rapid weight changes are often vulnerable to loneliness, fat-shaming, bullying inside and outside the home, sexual abuse, early puberty, or latent bed wetting. We will discuss these challenges and learn to create safe spaces for children to tell their stories, be heard, and receive the help and resources they need to have a healthy and happy childhood.

A recent study reported that children who are obese feel emotionally worse than those who are not, worse even than those undergoing chemotherapy for cancer. A sad yet true reality for so many children. If our children with too much weight gain too fast feel worse than a child with cancer, why can't we give each of them the same compassion to help ease their pain that we would give a child with cancer? How do we help children with too much weight gain feel cared for, loved—safe?

Our physicians often avoid the topic of too much weight gain too fast because they may struggle to find the appropriate tone and language to address it. And because the obesity epidemic affects everyone, some nurses and doctors with weight issues may be reluctant to talk about weight--just like us. Many doctors and nurses struggled when tobacco was proven harmful to us. Doctors and nurses who smoked were often reluctant to discuss smoking with patients! And why on earth would patients listen to a doctor tell them to stop smoking when the doctor had a pack of cigarettes tucked into the top pocket of their white coat?

Our children with obesity often face the stereotypes we all have heard: fat people are lazy, dull, bad at sports, and so on. These terrible prejudices create an environment where our children don't want to play with other children or prefer to do things alone. They become lonely. And sadly, they often experience bullying and insensitivity not just outside the home but inside it too.

Sometimes when we, even with our best intentions, attempt to address weight changes with our child, we may unintentionally contribute to feelings of depression, anxiety, low self-esteem, and poor body image. We can do better with our children. We must do better because the consequences are otherwise too significant.

Let's dive right in by understanding how you have learned to talk about your and your child's body. Complete the following activities by learning to reframe the words you use to talk about body, size and shape.

Here are a few examples of how we reframe an UNKIND thought into a KIND thought:

UNKIND words and thoughts

Big-bellied, lumpy, tubby

I have a big belly, and feel like a big lump. When I was a kid people called me tubby.

Reframing to KIND words and thoughts

Beautiful, round, well-suited, healthy

My belly is round and has beautiful folds. Its shape is well-suited to hold the food I need to eat to be healthy.

UNKIND words and thoughts
Thunder thighs, dimply, bumpy

My thighs are so big and bumpy, I hate the dimples. I get self-conscious when people talk about cellulite and cottage cheese thighs.

Reframing to KIND words and thoughts
Strong, powerful, useful

My thighs are strong and help me lift and carry my children.

UNKIND words and thoughts
Ugly, fat, unappealing

I feel so ugly when I gain weight. I'd be more appealing to others if I could just lose 20lbs.

Reframing to KIND words and thoughts
Attractive, accept, love

I will find a partner who loves and accepts all parts of me. My value and attractiveness are not based on my weight.

Reframing Activity

**Now it is time to reframe your unkind words to kind words.
Use this worksheet to begin reframing how you think about
you and your child's body size and shape.**

What words do you use to describe your body size
and shape? Write them here:

What words has your child used to describe their
body size and shape? Write them here:

How do you feel about your body size and shape?   Write
them here:

How do you feel about your child's body size and shape? Write
them here:

Now circle all the words that are kind.

Underline all the words that are unkind.

Reflect on the words that were kind and unkind. Did anything
shift in your thoughts and emotions? Describe it here:

At some point in your life, you have learned to think about your body type in this way. Maybe from your parents, partner, or the media images in our culture, or perhaps you were called these words at home, school, or at work. And you learned to accept the words and adopted them yourself. But here's the good news: anything you can learn, you can unlearn too. It will take some time to unlearn, but by learning to speak differently to yourself about your weight and your child's weight, you will be taking the first steps towards unlocking the power of kindness towards yourself and your child.

There are many adjectives we can use to describe human body types—I found more than 100 words we can use to think about our body type, which means that there are many we could choose. So let's decide how you want to talk about your and your child's body type. It is within your power to choose. It is within your power to share your selected words with people.

By people, who do I mean, and how does it work? People include your partner, your parents, your sister, your friends, your neighbors, your child's teacher, and your doctor. Frankly, anyone who comments on your or your child's body type can be corrected and informed of your preference. For example, suppose someone refers to your child as 'thickset' or 'chubby.' You can tell them that you prefer to express the positive things about your child's body—for example, she has strong arms or beautiful eyes, or her legs are flexible.

By doing this, you will learn to do 3 essential things:

- Learn how language affects your feelings—the power of words.

- Stay mindful of how you want to talk about your body type and your child's body type, and demand empathy and kindness for yourself and your child.

- Learn how to take unkind feelings or thoughts and begin to create environments where you and your child feel worthy of love and acceptance.

Consistency is essential in helping our children who struggle with weight-related issues feel less alone and more worthy of love and kind words. Changing how you speak about your body weight and size will directly affect how your child feels about their weight and size. Setting boundaries within and outside the family about how to discuss body weight and size will create the foundation for a loving, safe, and healthier environment for your child to grow and learn.

Below are several kind phrases to say to yourself and your child, to begin to change how your family talks about weight and body size. I am sure you can come up with more phrases that will ring true to yourself and your child.

Kind Things To Say To Yourself

- ❤ I will insist on empathy and kindness when discussing my body type.

- ❤ My body type is for me to determine, not others.

- ❤ I may choose not to discuss my body size or shape, which is okay.

- ❤ I may focus on my health, not my size or shape, which is okay.

- ❤ I'm worthy of loving-kindness.

- ❤ I belong wherever I choose to be.

Kind Things To Say To Your Child

- ❤ Just seeing you makes me smile. I'm so glad you are here.

- ❤ You are learning and growing—sometimes growing is fun, and sometimes it is hard. I am here for you when it's fun and challenging.

- ❤ No one is perfect, so let us be the best imperfect family we can be.

- ❤ I'm so happy we are a family.

- ❤ I think you have the most beautiful spirit when you _____.

- ❤ You inspire me.

- ❤ I cherish the joy and love you bring to our family.

- ❤ Hanging out with you is fun!

- ❤ I love talking with you!

- ❤ You are safe.

- ❤ You have good ideas.

- ❤ You can trust yourself.

- ❤ I like you!

- ❤ I love to hear your stories.

What is Shame, and How Does It Develop?

Let's start by clarifying what shame is and how it develops. It is a painful feeling arising from the consciousness of something dishonorable, improper, ridiculous, etc., done by oneself or another. Shame can result from comparing your actions with your standards. The roots of the word shame mean "to cover;" as such, covering oneself, literally or figuratively, is a natural expression of shame. When people experience shame, they may blush, become confused, look downward, lower their heads, and slouch. With intense shame, a person may become overheated, and their skin will blotch around the face and neck.

Shame can also make people cry. One of the key emotions in all forms of shame is contempt (Miller, 1984; Tomkins, 1967). When we feel shame, we feel flawed and inadequate and experience the effect of shame in situations of embarrassment, dishonor, disgrace, humiliation, or chagrin. When in a "state of shame," our sense of self is stigmatized, like being denigrated by caregivers, overtly rejected by parents in favor of siblings' needs, etc. To "shame" means actively assigning or communicating a state of shame to another. Behaviors designed to "uncover" or "expose" others are sometimes used for this purpose, as are utterances like "Shame!" or "Shame on you!"

Another way to think about shame is that it can prevent feelings of genuine concern from developing. The sense of being damaged is so potent and painful that it numbs your feelings towards anyone else. When we feel shame, we often idealize other people—they are seen as perfect, the lucky ones who live shame-free. This idealization can then turn into powerful feelings of envy—which leads to comparison and ranking behaviors. Do you allow people to hold you to a standard rather than appreciate your unique talents and contributions? Are you comparing yourself and your children to other families?

People who don't experience shame have parents who help them to develop a reliable sense of self. Their parents encourage them to view others as separate, yet they can feel concerned for them. People with limited experiences of shame will and do experience guilt—which is also painful. Still, there is a sense of wholeheartedness to be present, recognize that their actions may have hurt someone, empathize with that person's pain, feel remorse for having caused it, and seek ways to apologize or make amends. These are all signs of emotional intelligence that support feelings of worthiness rather than shame. In other words, with guilt, the self is not the focus of negative emotions; instead, the thing done to hurt us is the focus. Similarly, Fossum and Mason say in their book, *Facing Shame*, "While guilt is a painful feeling of regret and responsibility for one's actions, shame is a painful feeling about oneself as a person." When we let ourselves or other people make us feel bad about our size, shape, or weight, we are vulnerable to fat-shaming.

Fat-shaming happens when a person humiliates someone judged to be fat or overweight by making mocking or critical comments about their size, shape, or weight. Whether fat-shaming is subtle or overt—the intensity of the feeling of shame is often the same.

Here are just a few fat-shaming phrases we all have heard and may have even used ourselves, or with, or in the presence of our children:

OMG! I feel so fat.

Wow, you lost weight! You look great!

Do I look fat?

I can't believe I ate that whole bag of chips! They are going right to my thighs—and they are huge already!

I've absolutely nothing to wear. I've gotten so fat.

No, I can't eat that. I am on a diet. I need to fit into my dress for the party.

Wow! I can't believe she is wearing that! At her size!

Did you see how big that guy was? I hope I never get that big.

I can't believe you ate that whole bag of cookies!

When we use fat-shaming language, we stigmatize ourselves and our children based on weight, shape, or size. This feeling in a child of being disapproved when fat-shamed by parents, friends, classmates, or media images can cause future binge eating or other negative eating patterns. Fat-shaming in the home may also be bullying, a real problem for many children with rapid weight changes. Feeling vulnerable and unsafe because of bullying in the home can increase your child's risk for diabetes, heart disease, and stroke. Fat-shaming can cause children to feel poorly about their bodies and become depressed and stressed.

When our children or we absorb fat-shaming messages, it can shake our confidence and ability to make healthy changes. The shame we feel can turn into blaming ourselves, which can cause us to criticize ourselves because of our weight. In her study of more than 2,400 women with overweight and obese women, Dr. Rebecca Puhl at the Rudd Center for Food Policy and Obesity found that "79 percent reported coping with weight stigma on multiple occasions by eating more food, and 75 percent reported coping by refusing to diet."

Fat shaming is terrible for your health and does not, as some people believe, motivate people to lose weight. It will not encourage your child to lose weight. It can even cause you or your child to eat more to self-soothe. When we internalize fat-shaming messages, we turn off our rational selves, who know that weight is a complicated issue caused by behavioral, biological, emotional, and environmental factors. When shame burns inside us, we can forget that weight is not a reflection of our or our child's character.

8 Ways We Experience Shame

Recognizing Unworthiness

Avoiding people or places because you feel vulnerable to judgment

Wanting to be perfect

Isolating yourself because you feel unworthy

Wanting to disappear

Blaming yourself for everything, apologizing unneccessarily

Going overboard to please people

Making yourself small both physically and mentally

Feeling angry, sad, and unworthy of love and care

Fighting Off Feelings of Shame

There are a few ways to help yourself and your child fight off the feelings that fat-shaming produces. We can set specific and achievable goals to improve our health and be more confident to ignore, deflect or reject people who use fat-shaming language. We can also make sure our children are safe at school. A recent study found that 85% of 1,555 children reported seeing a child with obesity being "verbally teased and victims of physical aggression." The study also found that "while most students reported willingness to help a friend with rapid weight changes who had been teased, many remain passive bystanders in these situations, leaving their friends to cope with these experiences on their own." The study raised this question: How do we empower ourselves and our children with words and actions to create safe environments for children of all sizes? Which leads to the next topic—how do we talk with children about weight? Based on recent studies, there are solid arguments for and against discussing weight with children. Many findings are contradictory and differ based on the child's age and gender.

First, let's think about how we comfort ourselves, our children, and our friends when things aren't going so well. You may be thinking,"What does this have to do with talking with my child about their weight?" Let me show you how they are connected. You will need to be patient as I take you through this. If there weren't such terrible consequences from talking to your child about their weight in the wrong way, I could make this chapter a lot shorter.

To have genuine compassion for others, we must also have compassion for ourselves. Read this sentence again— *To have genuine compassion for others, we must also have compassion for ourselves.* When we speak negatively about ourselves, have regrets, and keep score of our or another's behaviors, we are not practicing compassion for ourselves. I am sure you can think of other ways you have not been kind to yourself, not your own friend. Think about a time you were hurting. What did you do? What did you say to yourself? What kinds of words did you use? Were the words kind, helpful words you would use with a friend in a similar situation?

I know the idea of self-compassion is not new. However, we humans need to be reminded of it —a lot! The Dalai Lama has written many books about compassion. Almost every issue of Oprah has an article with a self-care or self-love theme. So we must practice often and be reminded to look to others for help or guidance.

Special care is needed to comfort and stop the hurting when you or your child is in emotional, spiritual, or physical pain. Sometimes though, we unwittingly increase our pain or our child's pain rather than provide comfort. Knowing the exact right thing to say or do when your child is hurting can be challenging. Also, the circumstance may be a trigger for our past hurts and discomfort, adding another layer of nuance to the situation. As we try to comfort our children, we may end up making things worse. We pull away or recoil. We go to our rooms and isolate ourselves because we don't know how to help or don't want to make things worse.

What if, instead of trying to make things better and fix them, we just stopped and said to ourselves, "What do I need to feel loved right now?" Or said to our child, "What can I do to love you best right now?" By asking this simple question, we are staying present with the pain and discomfort and acknowledging that something is wrong, something hurts. We don't have to fix the problem this very minute—first, we must offer comfort. This isn't easy to do. We want to solve it. We want to ease our pain and our child's pain. By asking how best to be loved during discomfort or difficulties, we are saying, *"You deserve to be loved. You are worthy of love, no matter what is happening."* We focus on their well-being, empowering them, and acknowledging their wisdom. We know that ultimately, they will understand what is best for themselves; if they don't, we can help solve the problem later.

Comforting a child or ourselves back to a state of well-being by staying connected will prevent that terrible feeling of loneliness and isolation. Once you ask the question, be prepared for not knowing how to answer it. And that is okay—posing the question opens a space for many answers. And the answer may change—and that is okay too, especially if this is the first time you have asked this question of yourself or your child.

Establishing a space to care for your own and your child's well-being is essential to challenging conversations about changes in weight, health, body image, and sexuality. Be prepared for the answer to the question—it could be, "I need ice cream," "I need a new toy,' or "I need to be alone," or a combination of things. Following up on the answer to the question is vital to providing comfort and establishing trust.

What is the line between constructive criticism and shaming?

Your words are offering constructive criticism if:

♥ If you are choosing words that acknowledge your child's feelings.

♥ Your goal is to educate your child. Your intention is to teach.

♥ You are criticizing a behavior, not your child. You are doing so calmly, with kindness, and intending to educate and help your child.

Your words may be shame-based if:

💔 You are commenting on something a child cannot change, such as their size, body shape, eye color, height, weight, and personality type (shy, cautious, bold, brave, and so on).

💔 You are commenting on things that are part of a child's identity, such as clothing, hairstyles, makeup, and accessories.

💔 You are addressing a child's behavior publicly rather than in private.

Temperature Check Activity

A Temperature Check is one of the simplest activities we can do, but its potential to encourage a positive emotional state should not be underestimated. The Temperature Check is as easy as asking a single question at the beginning of the each day:

"How are you feeling today?"

Asking this question lets your child know that someone cares about how they are feeling. It also signals that sometimes they will be feeling something negative – and that's okay.

We can all use this reminder that we are human, which means that we are occasionally subject to emotions and feelings that we'd rather not have; however, this reminder can be beneficial for teenagers, who are likely dealing with more intense and varied emotions than anyone else. After asking this question:

❤ Encourage your child to ask *you* how you are feeling?

❤ Share with your child how *you* are feeling.

❤ Talk about your feelings *together* for two minutes.

Starting each day with this activity can get you and your child in the right frame of mind to be more kind and empathetic towards one another and alert you to potential problems.

The Worth Daily Practice Calendar helps record your family's progress towards creating a kind, body-positive environment in your home. Don't worry if you miss a few days here and there. Just hang it on the fridge or tape it to the wall by your child's bed and do your best.

WORTHY DAILY PRACTICE

WIND DOWN SUNDAY	FEELING SHARE MONDAY	LOVE U TUESDAY	SAFEST U WEDNESDAY	RAINBOW EATING THURSDAY	FEELING WORTHY FRIDAY	FILL UR CUP SATURDAY
How did U sleep?	How do U feel today?	How can I best love U today?	Where do U feel safest?	What green food will we eat today ?	What are UR strengths?	What do U like to do for fun?
How did U sleep?	How do U feel today?	How can I best love U today?	Where do U feel safest?	What red food will we eat today ?	What are UR strengths?	What do U like to do for fun?
How did U sleep?	How do U feel today?	How can I best love U today?	Where do U feel safest?	What yellow food will we eat today ?	What are UR strengths ?	What do U like to do for fun?
How did U sleep?	How do U feel today?	How can I best love U today?	Where do U feel safest?	What orange food will we eat today ?	What are UR strengths ?	How do U feel?

WORTHY DAILY PRACTICE

RECORD YOUR CHILD'S ANSWERS HERE

SUN	MON	TUE	WED	THU	FRI	SAT
	1	2	3	4	5	6
7	8	9	10	11	12	13
14	15	16	17	18	19	20
21	22	23	24	25	26	27

Review these word lists to help you have more meaningful conversations with your child.

Words To Help Instill Love in Your Child

#1 ADORE YOU
#2 DELIGHTED TO SEE YOU
#3 I CHERISH YOU
#4 I LOVE YOU
#5 YOU MAKE MY DAY
#6 I AM ALWAYS HAPPY TO SEE YOU
#7 YOU HAVE A BEAUTIFUL HEART
#8 YOUR SOUL IS SHINING
#9 I ADMIRE YOU
#10 YOU LOOK HOPEFUL AND HAPPY
#11 YOUR SMILE WARMS MY HEART

#12 YOU LIGHT UP MY DAY
#13 I'M YOUR BIGGEST FAN
#14 YOU MAKE ME LAUGH
#15 YOUR ARE SO MUCH FUN
#16 I'M ON YOUR TEAM
#17 I HEAR YOU
#18 YOU MAKE ME PROUD
#19 I BELIEVE IN YOU
#20 I'M LISTENING
#21 I'M ALWAYS HERE FOR YOU
#22 YOU LOOK NICE TODAY

FROM: HEPWORTH, D. H., ROONEY, R., & LARSEN, J. (2000). DIRECT SOCIAL WORK PRACTICE: THEORY AND SKILLS. PACIFIC GROVE, CA: BROOKS.

Words To Help Instill Strength in Your Child

#1 I AM CONVINCED YOU CAN
#2 SENSE OF MASTERY
#3 RESOLUTE
#4 STRONG
#5 BRAVE
#6 SUCCESSFUL
#7 IN CHARGE
#8 WELL-EQUIPPED
#9 INSPIRED
#10 SECURE
#11 IN CONTROL

#12 CONFIDENT
#13 POWERFUL
#14 DETERMINED
#15 INFLUENTIAL
#16 COMMITTED
#17 DARING
#18 IMPRESSIVE
#19 TRUST YOURSELF
#20 ON TOP OF IT
#21 SKILLFUL
#22 CAPABLE

FROM: HEPWORTH, D. H., ROONEY, R., & LARSEN, J. (2000). DIRECT SOCIAL WORK PRACTICE: THEORY AND SKILLS. PACIFIC GROVE, CA: BROOKS.

Words To Help Instill Happiness Your Child

#1 ELATED
#2 SUPERB
#3 ON TOP OF THE WORLD
#4 EXHILARATED
#5 DELIGHTED
#6 IN HIGH SPIRITS
#7 JOYFUL
#8 CHEERFUL
#9 GLOWING
#10 WONDERFUL
#11 ENTHUSIASTIC

#12 MARVELOUS
#13 THRILLED
#14 TERRIFIC
#15 HAPPY
#16 LIGHTHEARTED
#17 PLEASED
#18 NEAT
#19 FINE
#20 HOPEFUL
#21 FULFILLED
#22 CALM

FROM: HEPWORTH, D. H., ROONEY, R., & LARSEN, J. (2000). DIRECT SOCIAL WORK PRACTICE: THEORY AND SKILLS. PACIFIC GROVE, CA: BROOKS.

Words to help Instill Confidence in Your Child

#1 TRUST YOURSELF
#2 SHARP
#3 ADEQUATE
#4 CAPABLE
#5 CAN COPE
#6 UP TO IT
#7 EQUAL TO IT
#8 SELF RELIANT
#9 ABLE
#10 FIRM
#11 ON TOP OF IT

#12 IMPORTANT
#13 READY
#14 SKILLFUL
#15 WELL EQUIPPED
#16 BRAVE
#17 SENSE OF ACCOMPLISHMENT
#18 DARING
#19 IN CHARGE
#20 ON TOP OF THE WORLD
#21 PLEASED
#22 GRATIFIED

FROM: HEPWORTH, D. H., ROONEY, R., & LARSEN, J. (2000). DIRECT SOCIAL WORK PRACTICE: THEORY AND SKILLS. PACIFIC GROVE, CA: BROOKS.

Words To Help Talk About Loneliness With Your Child

#1 ALL ALONE IN THE WORLD
#2 ABANDONED
#3 ALONE
#4 LONELY
#5 LEFT OUT
#6 REJECTED
#7 SHUT OUT
#8 EXCLUDED
#9 LONESOME
#10 ALIENATED
#11 DISTANT

FROM: HEPWORTH, D. H., ROONEY, R., & LARSEN, J. (2000). DIRECT SOCIAL WORK PRACTICE: THEORY AND SKILLS. PACIFIC GROVE, CA: BROOKS.

Words To Help talk About Embarrassment With Your Child

#1 FOOLISH
#2 HUMILIATED
#3 MORTIFIED
#4 EXPOSED
#5 ASHAMED
#6 HORRIBLE
#7 DEMEANED
#8 EMBARRASSED
#9 FOOLISH
#10 GOOFED
#11 REGRETFUL

FROM: HEPWORTH, D. H., ROONEY, R., & LARSEN, J. (2000). DIRECT SOCIAL WORK PRACTICE: THEORY AND SKILLS. PACIFIC GROVE, CA: BROOKS.

Words To Help talk About Depression With Your Child

#1 DISHEARTENED
#2 IN DESPAIR
#3 ADEQUATE
#4 CAPABLE
#5 CAN COPE
#6 UP TO IT
#7 EQUAL TO IT
#8 SELF RELIANT
#9 ABLE
#10 FIRM
#11 ON TOP OF IT

#12 IMPORTANT
#13 READY
#14 SKILLFUL
#15 WELL EQUIPPED
#16 BRAVE
#17 SENSE OF ACCOMPLISHMENT
#18 DARING
#19 IN CHARGE
#20 ON TOP OF THE WORLD
#21 PLEASED
#22 GRATEFUL

FROM: HEPWORTH, D. H., ROONEY, R., & LARSEN, J. (2000). DIRECT SOCIAL WORK PRACTICE: THEORY AND SKILLS. PACIFIC GROVE, CA: BROOKS.

[4]

Learning Empathy, Compassion, and Kindness To Talk About Weight Changes

Empathy is a quality of character that can change the world.
—Barack Obama

There is a way for us to talk to children with empathy, compassion, and kindness about their feelings regarding gaining too much weight too fast. Let's take a closer look at the word kindness. How do we embody empathy, compassion, and kindness? What exactly are empathy, compassion, and kindness? How do we show empathy, compassion, and kindness?

Think about empathy, compassion, and kindness like this:

Empathy is when you can understand and care about how someone else is feeling.

Empathy is the thought.

Compassion is when you feel another's suffering and want to help relieve it.

Compassion is the feeling.

Kindness is the act of alleviating suffering, showing love, and being present.

Kindness is the action.

Empathy

Mary Gordon is an award-winning serial social entrepreneur in the field of education. She is an educator, author, parenting expert, and child advocate who has created programs informed by the power of empathy. Gordon beautifully describes empathy in this quote: "Empathy comes in many colors. Often we think of our ability to see from another's perspective as the essence of social intelligence. This cognitive form of empathy reveals how we make maps of others' minds to understand how they feel and what they think, and even imagine ourselves walking in their mental shoes. Others can also "feel felt" by us, sensing that their feelings are in tune with ours—that we resonate with their inner life. This form of emotional empathy enables us to feel close and comforted, to sense that others connect to us beneath and beyond logic and linear thinking of linguistic language. And even more, others can feel that we are concerned about them, have compassion for their pain, and take joy in their triumphs."

33

Responding to the feelings, needs, and desires of others is at the heart of the loving, healthy relationships that help us feel secure. As parents, your consistent presence and behaviors will help create circumstances for secure attachments to grow between everyone in the family. It's like the idea of harmony, having good reception on the radio channel, or being tuned in. If the tuner is off-channel, you are very aware of the static, the non-harmonious feeling in the room. Remember, empathy is about your child's ability to perceive and feel another person's emotions. Compassion is when those feelings inspire them to help.

How do we teach children empathy? We do so by helping them develop a moral identity. In a recent study, researchers found that children ages three to six who receive praise for helping others were less likely to act more generously in the future than kids who receive praise for being helpful people. We can help children develop a moral identity by sharing that they are thoughtful people who value others. It is one step beyond just praising them for good deeds.

So what does empathy look like?

Let's say a child shares a toy with another child when asked.

We typically say, "Good sharing" or "That was so nice of you to share."

Instead, we might say, "When you share your toys, I can see you care that others have a turn too."

So how do we know if we are helping our child develop empathy?

Here are a few signs that things are going well in a child's first six years:

Ages 0 to 2

By soothing an infant, you'll help them learn to comfort themselves and, eventually, to comfort others.

Toddlers are sensitive to their friends' feelings and often mimic their emotions, a necessary precursor to empathy.

Empathy must be repeatedly modeled and encouraged in toddlers before it becomes a part of their behavior.

Ages 3 to 4

Threes can make the connection between emotions and desires, and they can respond to a friend's distress with simple, soothing gestures.

Sometimes preschoolers can only relate to the feelings of others if they share the same feelings and perspectives on a situation.

Fours are capable of seeing a situation from another person's perspective. Yet they need to know that not all reactions to feelings are okay.

Ages 5 to 6

With their ever-increasing vocabulary, fives love to share their feelings. They can participate in discussions about emotions which will help them develop a better understanding of the feelings of others.

Fives and sixes learn to read others' feelings through their actions, gestures, and facial expressions—an essential empathy and social skill.

By modeling and encouraging empathy, kindergartners will learn to become compassionate members of a caring community.

Compassion

Compassion means "to suffer together." Emotion researchers say the feeling arises when you are aware of a person's suffering and feel compelled to relieve that suffering. Some people feel compassion in the heart, throat, stomach, or sometimes a combination of all three. When I feel compassion, it is typically in my heart and throat. It is as if my heart feels the pain I am seeing in another person, and then my throat tightens until I find the right words to say to comfort. Then my mind jumps in (empathy) and searches for the right words. I wait until I unearth the kindest words that won't diminish a person's dignity but lift their spirit and make them feel cared for. It is a balancing act, for sure.

Did you know that there are researchers who study compassion? One researcher, Dacher Keltner, the author of Born to Be Good and Faculty Director of the Greater Good Science Center, has shown that "when we feel compassion, our heart rate slows down, we secrete the "bonding hormone" oxytocin, and regions of the brain linked to empathy, caregiving, and feelings of pleasure light up, which often results in our wanting to approach and care for other people." So it makes sense that we can feel compassion in our bodies and get a boost of love when we act on them.

Where do you feel compassion in your body? As we better understand how we feel compassion, we can help our children learn too. When compassion motivates a child to act kindly towards someone suffering, we can reinforce that boost of love they may feel by praising their character, not the actual behavior. What does this look like in real life? Here is an example:

A child sees their friend struggling to put their boots on to play in the snow. We could say: You are such a helpful person. You saw your friends struggling and helped make sure they could be part of the fun!

Can compassion be taught?

In a recent study, Dr. Weng, University of San Francisco's Osher Center of Integrative Health trained young adults to engage in compassion meditation, an ancient Buddhist technique, to increase caring feelings for people who are suffering. In the meditation, participants envisioned a time when someone had suffered and practiced wishing their suffering was relieved. They repeated phrases to help them focus on compassion, such as, "May you be free from suffering. May you have joy and ease." Participants practiced with different categories of people, starting with a loved one or someone for whom they quickly felt compassion, like a friend or family member. Then, they practiced compassion for themselves and then for a stranger. Finally, they practiced compassion for someone they actively had a conflict with, called the "difficult person," such as a troublesome coworker or roommate. "It's kind of like weight training," Weng says. "Using this systematic approach, we found that people can build up their compassion 'muscle' and respond to others' suffering with care and a desire to help."

Remember, empathy leads to compassion which leads to acts of kindness.

How Do We Practice Self-Compassion and How Will It Help My Child?

To help your child be more compassionate, you must understand what self-compassion feels like for yourself. When we practice self-compassion, we can feel a warmth inside our hearts, a loving, patient, connected attitude that co-exists in our bodies and minds. As we learn to treat ourselves as we would treat a best friend, we can help our child learn too.

We can learn self-compassion in three steps:

♥ First mindfulness: As we tune in to our suffering, we can become aware of what hurts us and where it hurts. We can then name the pain. For example, I feel invisible and that no one cares about me. It makes my heart hurt, and tears come to my eyes. Acknowledge the suffering that you feel is difficult.

♥ Second, universal feelings: Think about others who may feel invisible, uncared for, and teary on any given day. What do you have in common with them? How is your pain similar? Can your suffering help you feel connected to others? Can it help you feel less alone?

♥ Third, being your own best friend: What would we say to a best friend who was feeling invisible? Uncared for? Ready to cry? Say this to yourself. Say it lovingly. When we tend to our hurts mindfully, we can begin to help our children do the same. Practice in front of your child; the next time you feel bad about yourself, say aloud, "I need to be kind to myself. I am so sorry, dear. You are doing your best."

What is a part of yourself you don't like?

Write it down here:

Now write a letter to yourself as if you are writing to your best friend.

How would you care for them?

What advice would you give them?

How would you offer your best friend compassion and kindness?

Research also reveals that doing good deeds, or kind acts, can make socially-anxious people feel better. For four weeks, a group of researchers from the University of British Columbia assigned people with high anxiety levels to do kind acts for other people at least six times a week. The acts of kindness included:

☺ Holding the door open for someone.
☺ Doing chores for other people.
☺ Donating to charity.
☺ Buying lunch for a friend.

The researchers found that doing nice things for people significantly increased people's positive moods. It also led to an increase in relationship satisfaction and a decrease in social avoidance in socially anxious individuals.

Acts of kindness create an emotional warmth, which releases a hormone known as oxytocin. Oxytocin causes the release of a chemical called nitric oxide, which dilates the blood vessels. Kindness reduces blood pressure; oxytocin is a "cardioprotective" hormone. It protects the heart by lowering blood pressure.

Here are some more ways to help teach kindness to children:

♥ Encourage their kind behavior for its own sake. Try not to link kind behavior to a reward. For example, do not bribe your child to share their toys. While it may be easier to get them to share, it can backfire: Kindness becomes something they do to get something. Instead, please help your child tap into that beautiful feeling that happens in our bodies after being kind. Help them understand that kindness is its reward.

♥ Reinforce their remarkable characteristics, not behavior. Research has shown that praising children for being kind encourages them to be kind people. For example, saying, "You're such a thoughtful person" instead of "That was such a thoughtful thing to do." Praising a child's character helps them see that kindness is inherent to who they are.

♥ However, we must thoughtfully criticize their behavior, not their character. According to Greater Good Science Center research, "It's okay to induce guilt but not shame. Children who feel guilt ("I did a bad thing") after wrongdoing are more likely to feel remorse and make amends than those who feel shame ("I am a bad person"). Criticizing a behavior conveys that the child can change their behavior and make better choices in the future. Such criticism may be especially effective when it includes positive affirmations such as, "You're a good person, and I know you can do better."

♥ Be a role model for kindness. When we model kindness, children will see it is a vital characteristic we value.

Now that you understand how we develop empathy, compassion, and kindness, try a few of these activities to cultivate kindness in your home, school, and the doctor's office.

[5]

Should I Discuss Weight Changes With My Child?

Since I don't look like every other girl, it takes a while to be okay
with that. To be different. But different is good.
–Serena Williams

Now that we understand how children develop empathy, compassion, and kindness, we can get to the hard part—talking with your child about gaining too much weight too fast. Quite honestly, this may be one of the most challenging conversations you have with your child. A recent survey showed that parents would rather talk with their children about sex than about weight changes. And there is a lot of pressure to get it right. So we will do that here. You will learn the best practices for discussing weight changes with your child; for example, you will learn which approaches may cause harm and which may help your child feel motivated, safe, and cared for. Here are two lists that give you the essential Do and Don't. I will share more about each throughout the chapter.

Let's begin with the 10 things you absolutely should NOT do to help your child become their healthiest weight. THE DON'T:

1. Don't tease your child about their weight or how much they are eating.

2. Don't single out your child and put them on a diet. Don't use the word dieting at all.

3. Don't talk about other people's weight, body size, or body shape.

4. Don't eliminate all unhealthy foods all at once.

5. Don't eliminate all screen time and social media use all at once.

6. Don't allow screens in the bedrooms. Screen use is best in rooms where you don't sleep, like the kitchen, living room, and so on.

7. Don't weigh your child every day or regularly.

8. Don't talk about specific parts of the child's body that may have become bigger or smaller with weight changes.

9. Don't compare your child's body to another child's body.

10. Don't talk poorly about your body, weight, and body shape.

The following ten things are what you should do BEFORE talking with your child about their weight. TO DO.

1. Do help your child feel comfortable in the body they have now. Be sure they have comfortable clothes that they feel good wearing. Compliment their clothing choices by linking what they are wearing to their personality traits, not whether the clothes make them look slimmer or hide their weight. For example, "That jacket is perfect for you. The style fits your fun personality." Or, "That dress is perfect for you. The style shows off how much you like springtime and flowers!"

2. Do make being healthier a family goal. Begin slowly to eliminate unhealthy snacks and foods. Try substituting one unhealthy food for a healthy one each week. Make healthy eating a yearly goal, not an immediate goal. For example, buy seltzer instead of soda for one week and sweeten it with natural fruit like a slice of orange or a frozen strawberry.

3. Do focus on your child's health, not their weight, body size, or body shape. For example, if your child is eating quickly, try saying something like, "Wow, you must be starving to eat that fast. Let me get you a glass of water. It will help you eat slower, digest your food better, and enjoy your meal."

4. Do actively look for any 'positive actions' your child may be taking to be healthier. Praise those behaviors and do them yourself as well.

5. Do reduce your own screen time before asking your child to do so. Make a goal to reduce your screen time by 10% each month for the year. Show your child your phone and how much screen time you are using, and then write down your usage goal and put it on the fridge. Each week share your progress with your child.

6. Do make a bedtime schedule for the entire family, including yourself.

7. Do find a date on the calendar to do a free, fun activity together as a family. Have a puzzle night, take a family hike, dress up for breakfast, play charades, try a new recipe, hold a dance party, walk around the block, plan a game night, and so on.

8. Do love yourself right now. Try saying, *"I love everything about me. Being healthy is my priority."* Whisper it if you need to, then work up to saying it aloud. Let your child hear you. Smile when they look at you with surprise and awe!

9. Do take things slow. Make only one change at a time until it becomes a habit, then commit to another healthy change.

10. Do avoid the scale—weight, body shape, or body size do not determine whether we are healthy or not healthy.

It is essential to consider your well-being and state of mind before trying to help your child. I know that sounds simple, but as you can see from the list above, there is a lot of planning before you talk with your child about their gaining too much weight too fast. The 10 To Do Now list can feel overwhelming. I get it. My best advice is to choose one thing to concentrate on each week for ten weeks. It is better to be prepared in ten weeks to have the best conversation you can have with your child. Better than to rush it and discuss their gaining too much weight too fast without preparing, which can risk leading your child to feel shame, uncared for, or unworthy of loving-kindness.

Being prepared is the kind thing to do.

Taking time to make health a priority in your life is the best path towards success in helping your child learn how to be the healthiest weight with happiness and acceptance. Say to yourself right now: *Living my healthiest life is my priority.*

Look over THE DON'T list. Are you doing any of the things listed on THE DON'T list? If so, write them down here.

Now reflect on how you can best stop doing THE DON'T. For example, if you have been weighing your child regularly. How will you stop doing this? You may simply stop weighing your child. You may put the scale in a closet, away from view. You may throw your scale in the garbage. If your child asks to be weighed, you can say our weight is only one factor in our health. I am trying to focus on our overall health. And leave it at that. Write down as many ways as you can think of for you to stop doing the things on your THE DON'T list.

Now, look at the TO DO list. Arrange them in an order that makes sense to you. Maybe making a bedtime schedule for everyone feels like a huge mountain to climb. How can you break it down into a more manageable task? I can't stress enough how important sleep is to being your healthiest weight. It may be the hardest of all things to do, but if you can commit to practicing good sleep hygiene and modeling it for your child, you will see the benefits fairly quickly.

Your sleep plan may look something like this:

I will set a realistic bedtime and stick to it every night.

I will keep light levels low in bedrooms.

I will invest in creature comforts like a supportive mattress, memory foam pillows, and good thread count sheets.

I will remove all screens from the bedroom: televisions, computers and tablets, cell phones, and other electronic devices.

I will try not to eat large meals or caffeinated beverages like teas and sodas.

I will try to exercise during the day.

I will try doing gentle yoga and meditation or listening to soothing music in the evening.

Using Your Own Words to Write Your Script

Now it is time to write your own script. Think back to the 'kind' words you used to describe your child's body, size, and shape. This is where you begin. Write them down here.

You may be trying hard to write your script now and can't get it right. No worries! Here is a general script in case you struggle to write your own. After reading the script, see if there are words or phrases your family uses that you can add to it to make it your own. Delete what doesn't fit your style.

WORTHY SCRIPT

Kind~True~Balanced~Necessary

We need to have a difficult conversation, is this a good time for you?

First, I want to share that you are---

I love you very much.

I am grateful we can make time to talk about this important issue.

I am concerned about---

I am worried that---

Can you share how you feel about---

I 'd like to discuss making the following changes this year so you feel safe and loved---

I know it will be challenging for us because---

However, I know we are strong and can do hard things like---

I want you to be healthy and happy and feel worthy because---

What will be the hardest thing for you---

What will be the easiest thing for you---

We will know if we need help if---

We will know we are successful when---

I love you.

WORTHY SCRIPT

Kind~True~Balanced~Necessary

Write your script here.

_____

_____

_____

_____

_____

_____

_____

_____

_____

_____

_____

_____

1. Read your script aloud.
2. Practice your script with a trusted partner.
3. Reflect: What went well? What felt awkward? What can you change?
4. Take a few minutes to revise your script.
5. Practice your script in the mirror. Check your body language.
6. Tuck your script away until you are ready to talk with your child.

♥ Keep an even, neutral, kind tone.

♥ Make eye contact, and don't be distracted.

♥ Make sure they are ready to talk. Ask them.

♥ Choose a private place and time.

♥ Tell them that the topic is challenging and that you may need to talk about it more than just now.

♥ Focus on health issues, not weight.

♥ Focus on behavior changes that are reasonable, suitable for their age, and that you can accomplish together.

Talking with children about weight gain is tricky. According to Marlene Schwartz, a psychologist and the Director of the Rudd Center for Food Policy and Obesity, "Even gentle prodding about weight isn't a good idea, in my opinion." Research backs this up: In one 2017 study in the Journal Eating and Weight Disorders, researchers found that women who remembered their parents commenting about their weight in childhood reported greater dissatisfaction with their bodies well into adulthood — regardless of their actual body mass index."

Hopefully, you have started making your home environment a place where everyone feels more optimistic about their bodies and worthy of loving-kindness. And you are prepared for the talk, with your script written in balanced, kind, necessary, and true words. As a parent, you need to be prepared by being clear about your intent, considerate of the timing, and having a good understanding of your child's social and psychological development.

With that said, it is my opinion, and that of a growing number of experts, that we can discuss weight changes effectively with children. When we fail to kindly and compassionately discuss a child's weight changes, we may neglect a vital development experience. And sadly, our silence does not protect them from bullying, feelings of unworthiness, social isolation, or sexual predators who may perceive them as older than their biological age due to early puberty.

What is most concerning is the relationship between bullying and suicide, especially in youth with obesity. Children with weight-related teasing or who experience bullying are two to three times more likely to report thoughts of suicide or to engage in self-harming behavior, such as cutting. An alarming statistic!

Children who have gained too much weight too fast are vulnerable to weight-related stereotypes, social exclusion, and discrimination. Often they experience bullying and insensitivity not just *outside* the home but *inside* it too. When parents, even those with the best intentions, attempt to address weight gain with their child, they may unintentionally contribute to feelings of depression, anxiety, low self-esteem, and poor body image.

8 Practices For Discussing Weight Changes With Children

Use Kind, Necessary, Balanced, and True Words

Be Prepared

Keep it Casual, But No Jokes

Focus on feelings and behaviors, not body size or shape

Notice Nonverbal Communication

Acknowledge Weight Bias and Body Shaming Environments

Help Your Child Share Their Feelings

Take a Whole Family Approach

[6]

Five Ways To Help Your Child Be Their Healthiest Weight

The healthiest response to life is joy.
— **Deepak Chopra**

Let's take a deeper dive into these five things. I have chosen each criterion for specific reasons that are important for you to understand. I have prioritized the five things to address the childhood obesity epidemic, the youth suicide epidemic, and the impact the Covid-19 pandemic is having on families.

Here are the five things you can do to help your child be their healthiest self:

♥ Support your child in having or finding a best friend.

♥ Make sleep a priority.

♥ Create time and space for your child to move often and freely.

♥ Set productive boundaries to help your child feel safe at home, at school, and at the doctor's office.

♥ Make a family commitment to buying, cooking, and eating healthier foods most days.

#1 Support Your Child in Having or Finding a Best Friend

Those who feel lovable, who love, and who experience belonging
simply believe they are worthy of love and belonging.
–Brene Brown

Why is it essential for your child to have or find a best friend? And why is it the very first thing I recommend? Children need to be heard, seen, and celebrated. A best friend will help your child feel heard, seen, and celebrated. A best friend is critical to helping your child feel included, loved, and appreciated. Children need the attention of others their age. They need to feel that someone likes them just for who they are. Children need safe spaces to play together, joke around, share stories, and just be themselves. A best friend helps a child who has gained too much weight too fast feel more secure, feel loved, and feel like they have one person in the whole world who gets them.

A best friend can potentially reduce your child's risk of experiencing bullying behaviors from other children. A best friend can help reduce your child's risk for suicide ideation or death by suicide. I know that is difficult for parents to hear, but as a society, we are facing a youth death by suicide crisis.

What is the link between a child gaining too much weight too fast and youth suicide? It is complex, just like everything else we are talking about in this book; however, here are just a few profoundly troubling statistics that informed my decision that a child who has gained too much weight too fast should have a best friend as a priority.

- Death by suicide in the U.S. is at a 50-year high.

- Death by suicide is the second leading cause of death for children ages of 10 and 19.

- According to a recent study published in The Journal of the American Medical Association Pediatrics, sadly, suicide attempts by children increased from 580,000 in 2007 to 1.12 million in 2015.

- It is heartbreaking that the average age of a child at the time of the Journal of the American Medical Association Pediatrics study was 13 and that 43 percent of the visits to the emergency room were for children between 5 and 11.

How to Help Your Child Have a Best Friend

If your child is struggling to make friends, it may help to try some coaching at home. Let your child practice being a friend with you. Talk about what friends do for each other and how friends resolve conflicts. Emphasize taking turns and sharing and explain that friends expect the same good behavior.

Ask your child what things they would like to do with a friend, and then help them understand the behaviors and traits they will need to do those things with a friend. For example, if a child wants a friend to play games with, you will talk about the importance of taking turns during a game, following the game's rules, and how to be a gracious winner and loser.

★Supervised Playdates

- ✦ Help your child choose a friend to invite for a playdate. Spend some time before the playdate going over expectations and hopes.

- ✦ Ask your child how they will help their guests feel comfortable. Share your ideas of what it means to be a good host in your home.

- ✦ Plan some activities with your child with some approximate times for each game. Help your child plan for transitions and for when it's time to move on to the next activity.

- ✦ Help your child notice if your guests are enjoying themselves. Are they smiling? Laughing? Do they look relaxed?

★Help Your Child Know Themselves

- ✦ Please help your child better understand themselves so they can choose friends wisely. Ask them what kinds of things they like to do.

- ✦ Please have your child practice introducing themselves and a few things about themselves.

- ✦ When children know themselves well, they are more likely to have successful relationships with like-minded children.

★Remember, Every Child Is Different

- ✦ Children need one or two healthy and meaningful friendships to be happy. It's vital that grownups not place too many of their own social needs on children.

#2 Make Sleep a Priority

It's very important that we re-learn the art of resting and relaxing. Not only does it help prevent the onset of many illnesses that develop through chronic tension and worrying; it allows us to clear our minds, focus, and find creative solutions to problems.

–Thich Nhat Hanh

Sleep is the next best thing to focus on when a child has gained too much weight too fast. Poor sleep habits increase children's risk of gaining too much weight too fast. Sleep loss creates a hormone imbalance in the body that promotes overeating and weight gain. Leptin and ghrelin--hormones that regulate appetite--production are altered in a way that creates increased feelings of hunger. Sleep deprivation is associated with growth hormone deficiency and elevated cortisol levels, leading to obesity. If your child struggles to make the recommended hours of sleep for their age, this may affect their ability to learn, remember things, deal with stress, and handle emotions.

The first step is to talk with your child about how sleep helps them be their best selves. Parents can show children that sleep is important for everyone by setting a family bedtime for everyone, including themselves. Make bedtime a natural part of the day by keeping time for bed messages positive.

Help your Child Sleep Well

- ☽ Make a plan together. Please write it down and post it near your child's bed.
- ☽ Make time for loving-kindness—some children like the extra attention during bedtime routines.
- ☽ Unplug. If possible, remove all screens from the bedrooms and keep them in a common area. Use bedrooms for sleeping, not places to use electronics.

Remember, Kindness is Key

- ♥ Keep it positive no matter how often your child gets up after bedtime.
- ♥ Kindly walk them back to their room with positive statements: *You will be so happy tomorrow to have the energy to do all the things you want to do. I can't wait to hug you in the morning. When you are well rested, things are easier for you.*

The Link Between Poor Sleeping & Weight Changes

Do you hear your child when they are sleeping? Snoring, heavy or noisy breathing and gasps for breath are all signs that they are not getting a good night's rest. If your child has gained too much weight too fast, they may have difficulty breathing, which can leave them tired, irritable, and unable to think clearly during the day.

Here is a list of several types of breathing problems:
• Snoring
• Restless sleeping
• Heavy or noisy breathing
• Sleeping sitting up
• Frequent waking during the night
• Sleep apnea

Here is a list of the daytime symptoms caused by breathing problems:
• Morning headaches
• Daytime tiredness
• Napping
• Poor school performance
• Inattentiveness
• Short-term memory loss
• Irritability
• Increased blood pressure

If your child is not sleeping well, make an appointment with your doctor. After an examination, the doctor may suggest your child go to a sleep clinic to be correctly diagnosed. At the sleep clinic, your child will be observed sleeping overnight. Sleep apnea can usually be diagnosed in one night, while other problems may take several visits. Your child will sleep with electrodes attached to them at several points on their body. A computer will read their brain waves, eye movements, muscle tension, and breathing patterns. The clinicians will also usually film your child sleeping. After the visit, a doctor will analyze the computer readings and the film and help you develop a sleep plan for your child.

4 Types Of Rest

**Sleeping and resting are different.
Practice resting.**

Active Physical Rest

Yoga, stretching, Tai Chi or any movement that improves your circulation and flexibility.

Mental Rest

Take short breaks to look out a window, daydream, listen to a song.

Sensory Rest

Turn down the lights. Close your eyes. Breath deeply for 5 minutes.

Emotional Rest

Say no when your plate is full. Make your health and spirit a priority.

3 Moves Often and Freely

We make the choice to rely on each other and believe in the radical potential of movement. Strong enough to be self-reliant and brave enough to ask for help. Hustlers, you don't have to do it all alone!
— Robin Arzon

Raising healthy children is challenging. And one of the biggest challenges many parents face is getting their children to move often and freely. The Centers for Disease Control recommends that children ages 6-17 move 60 minutes daily. However, only 1 in 5 adults and 1 in 5 students fully meet physical activity guidelines. Many families have a difficult time prioritizing movement for many reasons. Some families don't live in safe places for children to play alone or unsupervised outdoors. Other families are busy trying to make ends meet and working during the hours when parks and playgrounds are open. Many schools struggle to help children meet the requirements as well.

Every community is different. Playing outdoors is not always an option for children. We can encourage your child to play outdoor games inside, like hopscotch or Chinese jump rope.

Dance parties, online children's body movement or kid's yoga, Simon Says, sock skating, hallway bowling, balloon ball, and stuffed animal races are just a few indoor games to get kids moving and having fun. Be spontaneous. Encourage your child to run, skip or hop for just five minutes several times a day.

How to Help Your Child Choose Their Own Way to Move

If your child struggles to find ways to move that they enjoy, talk about it with them. Ask them what they don't like about a specific activity, movement, game, or sport. Even a short burst of physical activity can help your child build confidence and find out what they like to do. They don't need to join a soccer team! You can show your child that moving is fun by introducing them to various kinds of movement. Make family body movement time a natural part of the day with kind and encouraging words.

Some children who have gained too much weight too fast may not feel comfortable moving in public spaces. They may have been teased in the past about how they move. Also, some children become uncomfortable quickly when overheated from exercise. They don't like to be sweaty and hot. If possible, invest in purchasing well-fitting, lightweight clothing for your child. There are many different kinds of garments such as cooling shirts that reflect sunlight, moisture-wicking socks, and lightweight running shorts. The more comfortable they are in their clothes, the more likely they are to enjoy an activity, game, or sport.

Moving, Even When It's Hard

Find a new activity and set a time limit.

Focus on the Heart

Ask your child, "What do you wish you could try?"

Fun is Best

Plan for fun. Use positive language about trying something new.

Time Limit

Let your child do the activity for a short period of time and if they like it, they can do it longer next time.

Check In

Check in with your child. Did they enjoy the activity? Do they want to do it again?

#4 Feels Safe At Home, At School, and At the Doctor's Office

The only way to solve the weight problem is to
stop making weight a problem – to stop judging ourselves and others by our size.
Weight is not an effective measure of attractiveness, moral character, or health.
The real enemy is weight stigma, for it is the stigmatization and fear of fat that causes
the damage and deflects attention from true threats to our health and well-being.
— Linda Bacon

Helping Your Child Feel Safe At Home

If a sibling, extended family member, or co-parent is bullying your child, you must talk about it with your child and let them know you will protect them. Sibling bullying is "repeated aggressive behavior between siblings intended to inflict harm." Keeping kindness toward one another's family motto can help lessen bullying. If you hear or witness sibling bullying, stop it, then address the bullying behavior with each child privately and calmly. Praise your children equally to encourage kindness and avoid jealousy.

Helping Your Child Feel Safe At School

A recent study in The Journal of Depression and Anxiety reported that "approximately 160,000 children a day stay home from school because they are afraid of being bullied—that's over 3 million students per month." Children who are bullied are more than 2.5 times more likely to attempt suicide or die by suicide. Experiences of weight stigma also dramatically impair quality of life, especially for youth. A landmark study by Schwimmer et al revealed that children and adolescents with severe obesity had quality-of-life scores worse than age-matched children with cancer.

Furthermore, the manifestation of weight stigma is not isolated to older adolescents with severe levels of weight changes because negative weight-based stereotypes toward children who gained too much weight too fast emerge as young as three years old.

If your child struggles with bullying behaviors from another child at school, it is crucial to get the school involved immediately. Schools have anti-bullying policies that can help you make a plan to keep your child safe at school. Ask your child specific open-ended questions about any bullying experiences at school. It may help them open up and talk about it.

Here are some examples of open ended questions you can ask your child:
Has anyone ever bothered you in the stairwell?
Do you feel safe in the locker room?
Are your teachers in the hallways during class changes?
Do you ever see anyone being bullied by another student?

If you suspect your child is being bullied, encourage them to talk about it. Reassure them you will do everything in your power to stop it. Stay calm. Do not overreact. Create a team of people to help your child that includes: neighbors, teachers, school principals, friends, parents, and bus drivers. Create a circle of protection around your child while the bullying behavior is addressed.

Helping Your Child Feel Safe At The Doctor's Office

If your child is reluctant to go to the doctor's office, it may be because they are experiencing weight stigma. Weight stigma is defined as the societal devaluation of a person because they have excess weight. It often includes stereotypes that the person is lazy, unmotivated, or lacking in willpower and discipline. These stereotypes are harmful and lead to prejudice, rejection, and discrimination.

Research has shown that many doctors believe children with excess weight won't follow their orders and lack self-control. A 2012 study of over 2,200 physicians, researchers found that most doctors harbor significant prejudice against patients with obesity. When researchers surveyed almost 2,500 people about weight discrimination, women reported that doctors were the most common source of stigma about their weight.

Insisting on high-quality care from your doctor's office will help your child as an adult. Children affected by obesity are also more likely to have the following challenges with the quality of care when they become adults. They may avoid preventive health services and exams like cancer screening tests. Because of the weight bias at many doctor's offices, they may cancel or delay appointments.

It is essential to monitor your doctor's attitude, words, and behavior towards you and your child to help your child feel safe at the doctor's office. If a doctor's words harm rather than heal, you may consider finding a new doctor.

Weight Stigma & Children

Best Practices for Weighing Children

Doctor's Office

Ask the doctor or nurse whether being weighed is a medical necessity?

School

At school request that your child be weighed privately and turned around, so the number on the scale is not visible.

Home

Avoid weighing your child at home. If you do need to weigh your child, have them turn around so the number on the scale is not visible.

On The Scale

If your child does see the number on the scale, turn it into a positive. "You are 150 pounds of [name their best characteristics]. Your kind words are powerful.

5 Make a family commitment to buying, cooking, and eating healthier foods most days.

All good food comes from the earth. And whether you get that food from a farmers' market, your local grocer, or your own backyard, this I know for sure: The pure joy of eating well is worth savoring.
–Oprah Winfrey

There are many options for learning to cook and trying to eat healthier foods. And it can be pretty confusing which foods are the best option for your family to eat. Working with your pediatrician to make the right food choices for your family is best. Your pediatrician can connect you to experts such as a registered dietitian or community resources such as hands-on nutrition education and cooking programs.

The main thing I have learned from all of my research is that we need to help children choose healthy foods that reduce or prevent inflammation in their bodies. Recently the National Institutes of Health reported a rise in obesity-related cancers in young adults. There are many theories as to why this is happening. Some research points to an association between childhood or adolescent obesity and increased risk of colorectal, endometrial, and pancreatic cancers and multiple myeloma.

You may be wondering what the link between cancer and inflammation is. It works like this. When a child's body is in a state of chronic inflammation, it can have abnormal immune reactions to normal tissues or conditions such as obesity. Over time, chronic inflammation can cause DNA damage that can lead to cancer. Many processed foods, sugary foods, and drinks cause inflammation in the body. Consuming excess added sugar and refined carbohydrates cause several changes in the body, which help explain why a diet high in sugar can lead to chronic, low-grade inflammation.

These are the top foods that cause inflammation in the body:

- Refined carbohydrates, such as white bread and pastries
- French fries and other fried foods
- Soda and other sugar-sweetened beverages
- Red meat (burgers, steaks) and processed meat (hot dogs, sausage)
- Margarine, shortening, and lard
- Alcohol

One way to help your child learn about the link between foods that cause inflammation and put them at risk for cancer is the same way you probably already talk with them about sunscreen. Many parents are comfortable sharing with their children that they must wear sunscreen to prevent skin cancer. We can share our same concerns about certain foods that cause inflammation. Helping your child who has gained too much weight too fast choose non-inflammatory foods can move the conversation away from the idea that food is linked to our body, size, and shape or how much we weigh. Share with your child the benefits of a low-glycemic diet and that it can help your family prevent some cancers. Just like sunscreen helps your family prevent skin cancer.

Healthy Eating Options Quick Overview

Here is a quick overview of some eating options you may want to consider. Maybe one way of eating feels more intuitive to you, or mix and match various aspects of each way of eating. It could be fun to experiment with a few options as a family to learn about your child's preferences.

In the next section, I provide a brief overview of each eating style with links to various websites, such as Oldways, a food and nutrition organization that helps people rediscover the goodness of cultural food traditions. Here is a list of the styles of eating with the links to suggested websites to learn more, get resources, and download recipes:

Mediterranean Healthy Eating Option

African Heritage Healthy Eating Option

Latin Heritage Healthy Eating Option

Pacific Islander and Asian Heritage Healthy Eating Option

Native American and Indigenous People Heritage Healthy Eating Option

Ayurvedic Healthy Eating Option

Vegetarian Healthy Eating Option

Vegan Healthy Eating Option

Flexitarian Healthy Eating Option

Plant-Based Paleo (aka Pegan) Healthy Eating Option

The Nordic Healthy Eating Option

DASH Healthy Eating Option

Low-glycemic Healthy Eating Option

Mediterranean Healthy Eating Option

In the US, the Mediterranean eating option consistently ranks as one of the healthiest ways to eat to avoid many chronic illnesses. The Mediterranean diet is safe and easy to follow. It is heart-healthy and can help prevent diabetes. It also has been helpful to some people in achieving short-term weight loss and long-term weight loss goals. The Mediterranean diet is based on whole plant-based foods, including vegetables and fruit, as well as whole grains, legumes and nuts, with small amounts of animal products. Butter is replaced with heart-healthy olive oil, red meat is limited to no more than a few times a month.

In addition, sharing meals with family and friends is encouraged and an important part of enjoying the food you make. Studies suggest that this style of eating improves cardiovascular health and is associated with a reduced risk of cardiovascular death, certain cancers, certain chronic diseases and overall mortality.

African Heritage Healthy Eating Option

The African heritage diet is another science-based healthy eating option with positive health benefits. Why are heritage diets important to consider as an eating option for your family? According to Kelly LeBlanc, the director of nutrition at Oldways, an organization dedicated to sharing food and nutrition research, "Health disparities across the country highlight the need for more inclusive dietary messaging. African Americans are often told that the foods they grew up eating are unhealthy and that poor health is a part of their heritage. Oldways' African heritage diet pyramid, which was developed with guidance from leading African American nutrition scientists and culinary historians, flips the script by celebrating the culinary legacy and often-unsung cultural ownership of healthy eating for people of African descent." The African heritage diet is also steeped in cultural norms such as avoiding food waste and eating food that is in season.

The African heritage style of eating is very similar to the Mediterranean diet, as it's based on a variety of nutrient- and fiber-packed vegetables, fruit, grains, and nuts, along with healthy oils and seafood locally found in West and Central Africa, the American South, the Caribbean, and South America.

Oldways has an extensive list of <u>delicious recipe options</u> to plan a meal around African heritage cuisine. If you want to ease into this some of the foods found in this region of the world, here is a list of swaps:

African Heritage Diet Food Swaps

If you like...

- Spinach
- Arugula
- Pomegranate
- Cannellini Beans
- Eggplant
- Potatoes
- Walnuts
- Quinoa
- Salmon
- Hot Sauce
- Garlic

Try using...

- Collards
- Mustard Greens
- Passion Fruit
- Black-Eyed Peas
- Okra
- Yuca
- Groundnuts (Peanuts)
- Millet
- Red Snapper
- Harissa
- Ginger

U.S.News & WORLD REPORT

Source credit: Oldways

Latin American Heritage Healthy Eating Options

The Latin American Healthy Eating Option is flavorful, affordable, and has easy-to-prepare foods. Variations have traditionally existed in the parts of Latin America where maize (corn), potatoes, peanuts, and beans are grown, including modern-day Mexico and the other countries in Central and South America. This eating pattern is a blend of the broad traditional diets of four major cultures: the indigenous people (Aztecs, Incas, Mayans, and other Native Americans), the Spanish, and the Portuguese, and continental Africans. Foods to eat every day include fruits, vegetables, whole grains, legumes, nuts, and seeds. Fish and seafood are served twice weekly with moderate poultry, eggs, and dairy portions. Meats and sweets are served infrequently and typically are eaten on special occasions. Learn more about Latin American Heritage Healthy Eating Options here: https://oldwayspt.org/traditional-diets/latin-american-heritage-diet

Asian American and Pacific Islander Healthy Eating Options

The Association of Asian Pacific Community Health Organizations was designed to help Asian American and Pacific Islander Communities build nutritious plates with familiar fresh foods. On their website you will find information on portion sizes, nutrition facts, and tips to help individuals adopt healthier eating habits. Learn more about this eating style here: https://mhpsalud.org/portfolio/healthyeatingplateasian/

Native American/Indigenous Eating Options

Pre-European indigenous foods are local, seasonal, and healthy. There are no sugars, wheat (or gluten), dairy, or high-cholesterol animal products. In other words, they are not heavily processed foods with many fillers. The foods are naturally low glycemic, high protein, low salt, and plant-based, with lots of grains, seeds, and nuts. And they are delicious. Learn more about this eating style here:
https://www.bonappetit.com/story/healthy-native-american-diet
https://blog.opentable.com/native-american-dishes-chefs-restaurants/

Ayurvedic Healthy Eating Option

Ayurvedic eating style is based on Ayurvedic medicine which strongly emphasizes the importance of digestion as well as managing stress with meditation, yoga, or deep breathing. Ayurvedic eating style encourages eating a whole food, plant-based diet with healthy spices like turmeric, cumin, and fresh ginger that have anti-inflammatory effects and activate our digestive enzymes. The largest meal is lunch when digestion is strongest. Maintaining a diverse microbiome through a variety of local and seasonal foods is emphasized.

The Flexitarian Healthy Eating Option

Flexitarian is a blend of the words flexible and vegetarian, this eating style gives you more flexibility with vegetarianism. The eating style is mostly plant-based but does not eliminate meat products entirely (instead, it aims to reduce meat and saturated fat intake). It's a great way to eat more fruits, vegetables, nuts and legumes, which are important for overall heart health.

Plant-Based Paleo (aka Pegan) Healthy Eating Option

Similar to the Mediterranean eating style with its emphasis on fresh over processed foods, plant-based paleo takes it a step further by eliminating dairy, gluten, refined sugar and vegetable oils. While straight paleo also eliminates grains and beans/legumes, this version allows them in small amounts. Reframing how you look at meat (not as the main dish but as a side dish instead), eliminating highly processed and refined foods, and putting the emphasis on veggies as the star of the plate can help lower our risk of heart disease and many chronic illnesses. The pegan principle is a nutrient-rich diet that consists of about 75% plant-based foods, with the remaining 25% of your nutrition from animal sources. It stresses eating whole, fresh foods that are sustainably produced, with limited effects on the environment.

The Nordic Healthy Eating Option

The Nordic diet also has some research regarding health benefits, including lowering inflammation and risk for heart disease. It emphasizes the intake of fish (high in omega-3 fatty acids), whole-grain cereals, fruits (especially berries) and vegetables. Similar to the Mediterranean diet, the Nordic diet limits processed foods, sweets and red meat. This diet also emphasizes local, seasonal foods that can be obtained from Nordic regions. Of course, finding local Nordic foods may not be feasible for everyone, but I like the idea of eating more local foods and using what's available from our natural landscapes.

DASH Healthy Eating Option

The DASH diet, which stands for dietary approaches to stop hypertension, is promoted by the National Heart, Lung, and Blood Institute to prevent high blood pressure. DASH is easy to follow, and its recommendations are familiar. Eat fruits, veggies, whole grains, lean protein, and low-fat dairy. DASH discourages foods high in saturated fat, such as fatty meats, full-fat dairy foods, tropical oils, sugar-sweetened beverages, and sweets. Following DASH also means capping sodium at 2,300 milligrams daily, which followers will eventually lower to about 1,500 milligrams. A review of studies published in 2021 suggests that the DASH diet can help prevent high blood pressure, strokes, type 2 diabetes, and obesity.

Starting DASH doesn't mean making big changes right away. Instead, begin by making whatever small changes seem most manageable to you. The DASH diet website offers cookbooks, recipes, community support, and plenty of background information.

Low-glycemic Eating Option

Another popular diet is a low-glycemic diet. The Centers for Disease Control and Prevention (CDC) suggest that people with diabetes can manage their carbohydrate intake using the glycemic index. Sticking to a low glycemic index diet may help prevent conditions like diabetes and heart disease. However, it's not certain that this diet can help you lose weight any better or faster than a low-fat, low-carb, generally healthy diet.

What is a low-glycemic diet?

A low-glycemic diet can help you control your family's weight by reducing spikes in your blood sugar and insulin levels. Low-glycemic diets help reduce risks for cancer, heart disease, and other conditions. Eating a low-glycemic diet 80% of the time is one way to prevent being the food police and enjoy the holidays and special occasions foods. Denying children special occasion foods like cookies, candies, ice cream, and cake will make it harder to maintain an overall balanced diet. Helping your child balance the 20% of the time they eat foods that may cause inflammation will set them up for a healthy relationship with all foods. Here are some basic guidelines for eating a low-glycemic diet:

- Eat many non-starchy vegetables, beans, and fruits such as apples, pears, peaches, and berries. Even tropical fruits like bananas, mangoes, and papayas tend to have a lower glycemic index than typical desserts. Also, don't forget about frozen options, especially if you encourage your child to try new foods.
- Eat grains in the least-processed state possible: brown rice and whole barley, millet, and wheat berries; or traditionally processed, such as stone-ground bread, steel-cut oats, and granola.
- Limit white potatoes, bread, and pasta to small side dishes.
- Limit concentrated sweets—including high-calorie foods with a low glycemic index, such as ice cream—to occasional treats. Reduce fruit juice to no more than one-half cup a day. Eliminate sugar-sweetened drinks.
- Eat a healthful type of protein, such as beans, fish, or skinless chicken, at most meals.
- Choose foods with healthful fats, such as olive oil, nuts (almonds, walnuts, pecans), and avocados, but stick to moderate amounts. Limit saturated fats from dairy and other animal products.
- Eat slowly and stop when full.

If your child is struggling to like a variety of foods, talk about it with them. Ask them what they don't like about a particular taste, texture, smell, or food. Talk with your child about how food gives them the energy to do the things they like to do. Parents can show children that low sugar, low fat, and high protein foods are essential for everyone by bringing only those foods into the home. Make a family menu a natural part of the day by keeping meal times messages positive and encouraging.

No, Thank You Bites

Everyone is different. Please don't force your child to eat something they do not like. Encourage your child to take a 'no thank you' bite. Research from the National Center for Infant Toddlers and Families shows it can take up to 10 exposures to a new food for a child to decide whether they like it. Encourage your child to keep count of their 'no thank you' bites.

Try A Mindful Eating Practice

Make meal time a priority. Turn off the TV, cell phones, and radio.

Set the oven timer for 30 minutes. Eat your meal slowly with your child. Could you encourage them to chew their food? When the timer bell rings, dinner is over.

Remember, Kindness is Key

Keep mealtime discussions light and fun. Avoid talking about food issues or problems. Stay optimistic about the food that you prepare and the way it tastes.

Spice It Up

Is your child eating the same thing every day? Try new foods together, and it will make starting to learn mindful eating fun and interesting. Add new spices to vegetables, meats, and grains, such as cumin, curry, or garlic.

Let Your Child Be The Expert

Trying new foods together will make this step easier. Let your child take the first bite of the new food and then tell you about it. How did it feel in their mouth? What else did it taste like to them? Do they recommend you try it?

Frozen Is Best

When introducing new fruits and vegetables try frozen, instead of fresh.

Cheaper	Less Pressure	Quality Control	No Thank You Bites
Frozen is cheaper and last longer than fresh fruits and vegetables.	Frozen takes the pressure off of cutting up fresh fruits and vegetables.	Fresh fruits and vegetables go bad quickly and taste will vary.	Preparing a single bite of a food is easier and isn't as wasteful.

[7]

Keep Your Child Safe at Home, at School, and at the Doctor's Office

The boundary to what we can accept is the boundary to our freedom.
– Tara Brach

Parents impact their children's body image. A healthy attitude and kind, protective words can counterbalance biased remarks from people. Children who have gained too much weight too fast are vulnerable to receiving microinsults, microaggressions, microinvalidations, and microassaults from their family members, peers, teachers, and pediatricians.

Microinsults

Microinsults are often unconscious behaviors, remarks, or environmental cues communicating insensitivity, rudeness, or demeaning. These can include comments intended as compliments (e.g., "You're so brave" for exercising or wearing certain clothes") or visual cues that remind marginalized individuals that they are not respected (e.g., magazine covers that depict underweight women as the cultural standard of beauty).

Microinvalidations

Microinvalidations are often unconscious, though they directly erase or dismiss the lived experience of marginalized groups (e.g., claiming that racism is a thing of the past, dismissing the complexities of the obesity epidemic).

Microassaults

Microassaults are basically "old-fashioned" bigotry. They are often deliberate and reflect biased beliefs held by individuals who express them in covert or overt ways (e.g., using racist slurs and refusing to associate with people that are different than themselves). Microassaults tend to occur only when the offender feels safe expressing prejudicial attitudes due to anonymity or believing they are in the company of others with similar opinions.

Microaggressions

Microaggressions are most damaging because they exclude, negate, or nullify the target group's thoughts, feelings, beliefs, and experiences.

What can I do to protect my child from microaggressions and bullying behaviors?

Dr. Kevin Leo Yabut Nadal, a Distinguished Professor of Psychology at both John Jay College of Criminal Justice and Graduate Center at the City University of New York, has excellent recommendations in their Guide to Responding to Microaggressions. I have reframed Dr. Nadal's ideas for parents to address children's vulnerabilities to microaggressions and bullying behaviors.

- ✘ If I respond, could my child's physical safety be in danger?

- ✘ If I respond, will the person become defensive, and will this lead to an argument?

- ✘ If I respond, how will this affect my child's relationship with this person (e.g., teacher, doctor, family)

- ✘ If I don't respond, will I regret not saying anything?

- ✘ Does that convey that I accept the behavior or statement if I don't respond?

- ■ Assess, do you want to be heard?

- ■ Do you genuinely want to educate the other person and share that they hurt your child's feelings?

It is important to remember that your response as a parent will vary by context, situation, and relationship. Remember the power of kindness and gratitude in healing and strengthening relationships. Research-based approach by Dr. Diane Goodman, Social Justice and Diversity Consultant, suggests the following general approaches:

Ask For More Clarification

Could you say more about what you mean by that?

How have you come to think that?

What has happened that led you to believe that?

Share your process. I noted that you _____(comment/behavior). I used to do/say that too, but then I learned_____.

Calling In

I felt very uncomfortable with your comment. It's rooted in weight bias, and I wanted you to be aware of it.

Calling Out

What you just said is fat-shaming/weight biased/bullying.

(a person will most likely be upset—then name the emotion)

You are upset, but I can't allow that type of behavior/language around my child. It is wrong, and I want *us* to be and do better.

Online Strategies

We know that many children experience bullying behaviors by others online. You can offer to help your child be prepared for microaggressions and bullying behaviors in the following ways:

Teens--Help your child find a link to an article about microaggressions. Keep the link in a place on the computer ready to copy and paste into a comment or direct message. If appropriate, help your child follow up with a direct message to open a conversation about microaggressions.

Share with your child that it is okay to ignore microaggression if it helps them feel safe.

Encourage your child to Unfriend/Unfollow harmful pages that don't call out microaggressions.

Use Code Words

Adopt a family CODE word to use at gatherings when microaggressions, weight bias, weight stigma, or bullying occurs. When the CODE word is used, check in with your family members and decide whether to stay or leave the gathering.

Here you will write down your ideas for filtering out the body negativity that is part of your child's world and setting boundaries to maintain your body positive environment.

We call it a 'Back of the Pocket' statement that you practice to make it easier and faster to respond to body negativity comments.

Below is a short exercise to get you thinking about what words you will use to set productive boundaries at home, at school, and at the doctor's office.

When you have completed the exercise, print out the Back of the Pocket Statement. Carry it with you. Read it to prepare for times when you and your child may be vulnerable to body negativity discussions or situations. Practice your statement with someone you trust.

When someone comments on my child's size, shape or weight, I will say the following:

When my child is exposed to a conversation about people's size, shape, and weight, I will say and or do the following:

When my family's size, shape, or weight becomes part of a conversation, I will say and or do the following:

These Are The Kind Words I Will Use To Describe My Child

These Are The Attributes I Will Focus On To Describe My Child

What to Do if No One Is Helping Your Child
Who Has Gained Too Much Weight Too Fast?

Speaking with a child about their weight is just like speaking to anyone about their weight—your words need to be balanced, kind, necessary, and true. Also, caregivers must prepare by being clear about their intent, considering the timing, and understanding their child's social and psychological development.

When we fail to kindly and compassionately discuss children's weight gain, their feelings about weight changes, and how they are experiencing their weight and body shape, we may neglect an important experience in their development.

Children who have gained too much weight too fast face weight-related stereotypes, social exclusion, and discrimination. Often they experience bullying and insensitivity not just *outside* the home *but in it*. When parents, even those with the best intentions, attempt to address weight gain with their children, they may unintentionally contribute to feelings of depression, anxiety, low self-esteem, and poor body image.

Protecting Your Child From Bullying is a Priority

Sadly, our silence does not protect them from bullying, feelings of unworthiness, or social isolation. What is most concerning is the relationship between bullying and suicide, especially in youth with obesity. Children with weight-related teasing or who experience bullying are two to three times more likely to report thoughts of suicide or to engage in self-harming behavior, such as cutting. An alarming statistic! Hopefully, this book has helped you learn how to talk positively with children, their teachers, and clinicians about weight-related issues.

Communicating With Your Pediatrician

What You Should Expect

Monitoring	Assessments	Explainantions	Referrals	Compassion
Help you monitor your child's health and growth.	Assess your child's growth and development.	Explain your child's illnesses and treatment.	Provide referrals and work with specialists to help your child.	Communicate with compassion and use kind words.

[8]

Staying Hopeful

I believe that the most profound expressions of the human spirit derive from hope. –Anthony Scioli, PhD

We all go through tough times when we see the world as hopeless. When giving up feels more manageable than trying. Whether we have feelings of hopelessness related to traumatic events like the death of someone we love, a divorce, sexual trauma, or being bullied, or because our efforts to be a healthier family have failed— hope is a resource available to anyone and everyone.

These five practices will help you embrace a process that takes you from sadness and hopelessness to action and positive change. Fortunately for our loved ones, our livelihood, and our lives, there are a few tried and true things we can do to begin to practice and restore hope.

1. **Shift Your Expectations**

A self-fulfilling prophecy is real, and its consequences are just as real. When we believe something is not going to work out or be terrible, and then it doesn't work out or is terrible, it reinforces the loss of hope. When we make gloomy predictions and catch ourselves thinking the worst, this is good! We are aware of these thoughts and can interrupt the critic inside us. Try this: Find one thing—it doesn't have to be a big thing—a small thing is best— that could make the day better or happier. Things like appreciating flowers or a bird's song, inviting a coworker to lunch, or complimenting your child and helping them feel special. By shifting our focus, we can shift our expectations. We can feel more hopeful about our day by setting an intention to make our day better or happier.

2. **Build Your Own Story**

When things aren't going well, we can try to give them meaning, give them a story. We survived. How did we do it? What characteristics helped us survive? Build a narrative that ends with success instead of shame. Let's be beacons of hope for others. If we survive, they can too. Share your story. Spread hope.

3. **Get Out Of Your Head**

Try to reach out to someone and ask them to share a story about a difficult time in their life—when they felt hopeless. Ask them, how did you make it through? How did you stay hopeful? Then listen, hear what they are saying. Repeat back to them some of the essential points. Sometimes hearing others' stories can give us the courage to share our own or see them in a new light.

4. **Remember Your Home**

What do we love more than ourselves? Our family, our pet, our neighborhood, our faith, or even things like singing, creating, gardening, rock climbing?

5. **Where There's Life, There's Hope**

Stay connected to family, friends, neighbors, coworkers, or whoever is in your life. Do a kind thing for someone else. Or smile at the next person you see and say good morning. When we isolate ourselves, it fuels our loneliness, sense of being other, and feeling unworthy. Let's reach out for help, to ask for what we need. We know that hopelessness and isolation are closely associated with death by suicide. When we lose hope, we are susceptible to suicidal ideation. We can learn to replace fear and doubt with hope. However, hope can coexist with fear and doubt—we can feel all these things simultaneously. How we each experience hope is unique to us. Some people feel hope when they pray, others feel hope when someone treats them kindly, or some people feel hope when they see a bird take flight or share a good laugh with someone.

We can build hope in ourselves by making realistic goals and envisioning what it will look like to succeed. Before we begin to work on our goal, it helps to envision the path forward. What is the first step? What are the next steps? What is the last step? What is the contingency plan to deal with problems or challenges? When things don't go as planned, we need the fourth skill. We can learn to pivot or change our goals to stay in reality. Pivoting to change our goals can help us stay hopeful.

And finally, remember that humans are designed to grow and heal. And we can by staying connected, asking for help, reflecting on our choices, knowing we are not alone, and seeking professional care if a feeling of hopelessness persists.

Helping Your Child Feel Hopeful

When we answer our toddler's never-ending questions like "what's this?" or "why?" We are encouraging them to share their desires and foster hope. Here are five steps to foster hope:

1. **Time—Children Need Our Time**

A hopeful child is both optimistic and determined. One meaningful way to instill these qualities in our children is by spending time with them. When our children feel safe and secure early in life, it sets them up to have the confidence to try new things or to set bigger goals.

2. **Set Stretch Goals**

Stretch goals are small challenges that will build children's confidence. For example, set a goal for throwing a ball with your child. Keep it in the air for three throws, five, and seven. Then celebrate each small achievement.

3. **Encourage Brainstorming**

When we encourage our children to brainstorm solutions to challenges, it helps them try new things and learn from them themselves. When we rush to fix things for our children, we send a strong message that they are incapable. When our children experience failure, we can focus on the *strategy* rather than them doing something wrong. Hopeful children are curious and eager to take on challenges.

4. **Weekly Family Meetings**

Taking time to meet together as a family helps cultivate a sense of belonging and hope in our children. Family meetings are a time to check in with one another about what's working and what needs attention. Successful family meetings are fun and engaging, with everyone participating.

5. **Live It**

Children with at least one hopeful parent are more likely to be hopeful. A hopeful parent is busy planning new things for the family to try, openly discussing obstacles and challenges, and working towards something bigger than themselves. Our children watch us. Our children learn hope from us.

ACKNOWLEDGEMENTS

My heartfelt and deepest appreciation to everyone who helped Worthy become a book, a podcast, a newsletter, an online workshop and a trusted resource for parents and children trying to create body positive, healthy, loving homes.

Thank you Marie McCormick and Meredith Ligiori for your research support, creative social media communications, immense passion, talent and boundless good nature.

Thank you Linda Wagner for your brilliant editing, reflections, and support.

Thank you Elisa Mula for being a friend, supporter and sounding board during the early development of Worthy. I will always remember our long strategy and brainstorming calls and our willingness to help each other.

Thank you Eren Marten who provided crucial information about podcasting and following your passion. We spoke just at the right time. You showed up exactly when I needed your expertise and enthusiasm.

Thank you to the very first workshop participants who inspired me to keep going. Every week I was delighted to share and learn from you. You know who you are!

Thank you to Sheila Patel, Leslie Goldman, Akerei Maresala Thomson, Elia Chan, Benita Zahn, Mary Glen, Elyn Zimmerman, and Elisabeth Fontaine who helped promote, support, and believe in Worthy! I am immensely grateful and amazed by the impact of your work in the world!

Thank you to the following organizations that helped professionals working with families learn about the power of kindness in helping create body positive environments for children:
Colorado Society for Clinical Social Work
Independent Health of Buffalo New York
New York State Social Workers Association
New York State Public Health Association
New York State Association of County Health Officials

Evan Walden, to you I owe a giant thank you! You shared your knowledge, time, and enthusiasm to help me develop a sound strategy to bring Worthy to life.

My deepest thanks to Anastasia Schepers, a trusted sounding board and co-presenter, for her unyielding support and encouragement. I will be forever grateful for your friendship and most generous heart.

I am lucky to have a dear, wise, talented sister, Sandra Sculli, who inspires me on a regular basis. Thank you for being there for me always and for our long discussions about how to best bring Worthy to life.

Deep gratitude to all my beloved forever family members, the Steves, the Scullis, the Fowler-Fennellys, the Nelsons, the Glovers, and my faithful assistant and co-worker Daisy.

I offer deep gratitude and thanks to Noah Fowler, Lauren Glover, Ripley Jo Fowler, Rylan Nelson, Zoe Nelson, Tom MacGregor, Colette MacGregor, Camille MacGregor, and Lena MacGregor for offering their encouragement and love to me everyday. I am because we are.

Thank you Todd Nelson, who read *Worthy* countless times, provided early edits, and for his patience, love, and encouragement to take the time and space I needed to complete this work.

I want to especially thank Rudy and Shirley Nelson. They offered encouragement, generous funding, and their never-ending confidence in me to create Worthy.

And finally, *Worthy* was possible to write because of the tremendous resources and support I was afforded through my work with amazing, generous, and passionate researchers, physicians, nurses, social workers, public health professionals, foundations, and families. I was able to complete this work thanks to my therapists and counselors, mentors and beloveds along the way who loved and cared for me, and helped strengthen my voice, my heart, and my spirit. Thank you to each of you who have helped me feel worthy of loving kindness so that I am able to share my learnings with others.

This book is written with the hope of creating safe spaces for all children everywhere. May they feel worthy, loved, and safe.

Image By Stephanie LaMont Photography

JoAnn Stevelos, MS, MPH has dedicated her life to service and studying programs that respond to the youth suicide, bullying, and obesity epidemics. She has created a compassionate and holisitc program, Worthy: The Power of Kindness in Raising Body Positive Children.

Worthy gives parents of children who have gained too much weight too fast hope, practical advice, and real-life solutions. JoAnn has over 20 years of experience researching childhood obesity prevention programs. Her education includes a Master's in Science (Bioethics) from Albany Medical College, a Master's in Public Health from the State University of New York, and a BA in Liberal Arts from Columbia University.

Dedicated to working with people who lead with love and hope, JoAnn's approach to her public health work is informed by Dr. Gail Christopher's work that promotes truth, racial healing, and transformation as a path towards justice and peaceful co-existence. What she has learned is that often people who are vulnerable to public health epidemics feel isolated and are vulnerable to hopelessness, which has led her to become part of Dr. Anthony Scioli's Hope Institute. Hope is necessary for positive change and can be strengthened. And how to maintain hope in your family is something you will learn about in the *Worthy* program.

JoAnn has been the Director of the New York State Center for Best Practices to Prevent Childhood Obesity, as well as Director of Research, Evaluation, and Learning for the Clinton Foundation's Alliance for a Healthier Generation and Michelle Obama's Let's Move program. JoAnn is currently an international consultant for children's health and wellness programs. You can also read more in-depth articles in her blog for <u>Psychology Today, Children at the Table.</u>